PLAYING WITH M

OTHER TITLES BY BASIL DU TOIT

Home Truths, Carrefour Press
Older Women, Snailpress
From the City of Ideas, Touchpaper Press
Old, Smith|Doorstop
Gathering Photons in May, New Generation Publishing

Playing with My Christianity

Collected Sonnets
Volume Two

Basil du Toit

Published by New Generation Publishing in 2023

Copyright © Basil du Toit 2023

First Edition

The author asserts the moral right under the Copyright, Designs and Patents Act 1988 to be identified as the author of this work.

All Rights reserved. No part of this publication may be reproduced, stored in a retrieval system or transmitted, in any form or by any means without the prior consent of the author, nor be otherwise circulated in any form of binding or cover other than that which it is published and without a similar condition being imposed on the subsequent purchaser.

ISBN   978-1-80369-966-0

www.newgeneration-publishing.com

Playing with My Christianity, Volume Two of Collected Sonnets

UNIFORM WITH THIS VOLUME:

Gathering Photons in May, Volume One of Collected Sonnets

ACKNOWLEDGEMENTS:

Versions of some of these poems have appeared in the following publications:

Stanzas, The Lighthouse, Poetry Salzburg Review, Edinburgh City Council Pamphlet, Southlight, Studies in Khoisan Verbs, The Dawntreader

My thanks to all the editors who gave space to my poems in their publications.

I would also like to thank the colleagues and fellow poets I worked with for many years in the School of Poets writing group based in the Poetry Library of Scotland, Edinburgh; special thanks, love and gratitude to Tessa Ransford, Christine de Luca and Ann Gwilt.

The artwork on the cover is based on a pastel study called *Teapot from Ramallah* by Eve Ferguson. My sincerest thanks to her for permission to use this work.

I would like to dedicate this volume to my partner, Eve Ferguson – thank you for your generous and unfailing support in my pursuit of this project.

Edinburgh, Scotland
2023

Die kehlkopfverschlußlaut
singt

the glottal stop
sings

Paul Celan, *Fadensonnen*

CONTENTS

Understanding Poetry 1
Impulse and Direction 2
Elizabethan Love Sonnet 3
Our Personal Moons 4
A Second Human 5
Writing 6
Visibly Touched 7
Adrenalin 8
Earth-Collapse 9
The Difference 10
Bright Stipplings 11
Flushing Out the Game 12
Weather Masters 13
Spirals 14
This Object 15
Naughty Greens 16
Persuasion 17
Native Language Landscape 18
Trumpet Raspberry 19
Spring Epidemiology 20
Tarmac and Tapestry 21
Sonnet Hornet 22
A Food Amnesty 23
My Penitential Greens 24
Steeped in World 25
The Politics of a Dutiful Daughter 26
In His Own Image 27
Eyeballed by an Ant 28

Ennui	29
Descriptive Limits	30
Sleeping Swans	31
Flight Readiness	32
Brain Habitat	33
John Ruskin, *Blenheim Orange Apple*	34
Seasonal Euphoria	35
Crows Clowning in the Air	36
Exactly Ten O'clock	37
Snap	38
A Glass Sonnet	39
Fit as a Fly	40
Beef Cheeks and Cauliflower	41
Seceding Embodiment	42
Shatterproof	43
Ice	44
Albuminous Squid	45
On My Late Espoused Saint	46
Power	47
Tranny	48
Woman Reclining on a Leopard Skin	49
The Vagina	50
Well-Earned Growth Rings	51
Eating Squid	52
Acid Recall	53
David Hockney's *Arrival of Spring*	54
A Pragmatic Crow	55
An Insect of the Order Odonata	56
Lock Up Your Drawers	57
Close to Perfection	58
A Solo Wedding in Kyoto	59

Stiff and Salty Boots 60
Star Traveller 61
Tales from Plutarch 62
Mother and Daughter 63
Soft Enough to Eat 64
Winged and Wonderful 65
Palliatives for a Tormented Parliament 66
Time's Numbering Clock 67
Readers of God 68
A Tale from Ovid 69
Seeing Quince 70
Playing with My Christianity 71
Concrete Dipping Basin 72
Sound-Creep 73
Yeah! Yeah! Yeah! 74
The Fly is a Perfect Example 75
Country Proverbs 76
Aargh! 77
On the Train to Fish Hoek 78
Leafing Creeper 79
Out of the Forcing-Box 80
Wilkinson Sword 81
Dead Musical Trees 82
Transmission 83
Forces on Phrasal Texture 84
Atrophy and Regeneration 85
Crow Landing 86
Talkin' 'Bout My Generation 87
Performative Utterance 88
Engine Philology 89
Writing for the Mouth 90

Not Such a Pathetic Fallacy 91
Lessons in Baroque Decorum 92
The Locust Daughters 93
Ages of Apogees 94
Spelt 95
Lessons from a Native 96
Love Among the Over-Sixties 97
An Ambivalent Bequest 98
Bulawayo Sex Lessons 99
Mists and Fruitfulness 100
Dromedaris, Reijger, Goede Hoop 101
Right Ventricular Cardiomyopathy 102
Amplification 103
Voyages of Discovery 104
Tutti 105
Fishes in Books 106
Japanese Dagger 107
English in Africa 108
Urban Igloo 109
In/Out 110
Tangled in the Metaphysics of Time 111
Native to the Islands 112
The Pleasures of Reading and Classical Learning in China ... 113
Pleiade 114
Flip-Flop 115
The Real Work 116
Landing a Shit-House on the Moon 117
A Question for the Dawn 118
Cardiomyopathy 119
Gigolo 120
Exercise Regime 121

In a Hide 122
I Have Read *Watt* 123
The Common People 124
A Woman of Years 125
Return from the Islands 126
Homunculus 127
The Illusion Room 128
Navigation in Green Water 129
A Stoic's Injunction 130
At the Mercy 131
Cold and Crows 132
Comparative Religion 133
Life Brought into the House 134
Full Immersive Response 135
Weapons of the Friendly Islands 136
Vanishing Apes 137
A Common Road 138
A Glans Sonnet 139
Albertine Asleep 140
Metatarsus Varies 141
Dialect of the Tribe 142
In a French Field 143
Wedding Cemetery 144
Stone World 145
The Concept of Nature 146
The Earth Our Dwelling Place 147
Uit Die Hantam 148
Bird Feeders to the Rescue 149
Expunged 150
Suspicions of the Ancestral Ape 151
Raw Philosophy of Miracles 152

A Descent of Man	153
The Grass Campaigns	154
Mortarless Cities of Central Africa	155
Solar Alchemies	156
Pamela in Her Body	157
Ordnance Lost Overboard	158
Clarinet Dropsy in Dalmeny Kirk	159
The Fierce Wheat in Samuel Palmer	160
Lunar Theatre	161
Measures	162
Library Session 531	163
Shoes in the Charity Shop	164
Thousand Year Reigns	165
First Thing	166
Field Naturalist in Situ	167
Rough Gully Bash	168
Living on the Moon	169
A Posy of Smells	170
Mere Heavenly Walking	171
Initiation Rapture	172
Who Was the Prophet's Mother?	173
Poet to Social Worker	174
In the Thread of Compte	175
Like a South-Facing Window	176
Still Morning with Birdflight	177
Recollection and Vocabulary	178
OMFG	179
The Greatest Poverty	180
Songs	181
Satisfaction and Satiation	182
Direct Current	183

False Teeth and Hearing Aids 184
Ode to Industrial Bodies 185
On the Autism Spectrum 186
French Saxophone 187
A Pond of Lilies 188
An Imagined Resumption 189
Clean and Busy Seas 190
Creek Fishing 191
Potable Gold 192
The Suppliants 193
Susannah Soiled 194
The World as Will 195
Crow Theology 196
My Nefertiti 197
Vegetable Nature One Vast Parasite 198
Working-Class Jesus 199
Dreamed in Stertorous Sleep 200

AFTERWORD to *Playing with My Christianity* 201

Alphabetical Index 203

UNDERSTANDING POETRY

It's years since I gave up trying
to understand poetry; now I read it
just to hear the rustle of language
flowing by with the sound of wind
leafing through trees. I can't get enough
of the passage of words bubbling
along in their stream of grammar.
Sometimes I catch sight of a river crab
cornered, raising its defensive mitts;
or a pale frond of Australian wheat
takes my fancy, beaded with golden
drops of corn. I just can't be bothered
trying to get at the meaning of poetry
nowadays – I read it for the pictures.

IMPULSE AND DIRECTION

Thorny herrings split the sea
from shore to shore, passages
compelled by lodestones tugging
grains of magnetite in brains;
navigational charts run along-
side the dorsal line from gill
to rudder, sea routes tattooed
on the scaly skin; bone-work
as light as a bird's, engraved
with the Signs of the Zodiac,
gives their owners a head-start
on urchins, star- and jelly-fish;
their spines and prickly hackles
are laid back for amazing speed.

ELIZABETHAN LOVE SONNET

Her face is a corridor full of blue basins,
hat-stands and hall mirrors. Rooms lead off
to where bosomy arrangements of flowers vie
with heavy dinner plates to see who's whitest.
There's even a bedroom that's like a fall from
a ten-storey building, so compelling in its throaty
promises, hoarse oaths, grunted confessions.
A civilised piano tinkles in the gloom, stroking
the fur of some very unfriendly modern music.
There's something Iberian in her magnetism
(at this, the slot machine flung jackpot coins
about like a wet dog giving itself a good shake).
A college is dropping sweet gum into her mind
where clever books puff up like hothouse lilies.

OUR PERSONAL MOONS

Your moon was a gift from North Africa,
a bright lunar baby risen from the desert
yelling its ripe round fever at the night;
mine was a present from Fife, one as cold
as war-plate pulled from the North Sea,
chastening and tempering itself to white steel;
every moon is local, specific to a place –
it's almost the creation of a single room,
framed in a window, triangulated in the
trigonometric sums of two pairs of eyes;
there must be thousands of moons dotting
the sky at any one time, like a luminous
flotilla of pulsing, lacy jellyfish, each visible to
just one of us, as private as our own minds.

A SECOND HUMAN

Vegetation has bulked up the pathways
with lustrous blockings of plant-fibre.
The material and the inspired worlds
shine with the same light over comfrey
and sleek, long-necked, towering daisies.
A river slips by in its brown, oily music.
The eye more than notes – is entranced
by birds voicing their signature vowels.
But nothing suggests an awed avowal
that beneath these surfaces botany ends
and something more transcendent begins.
For the world by itself is not enough –
you must also be there, viewing it all –
muscle, brain, uterus of your solid body.

WRITING

The world, not so much in pill form
as in some kind of neurological state,
comes to me, filling me like an ark of
cargoes that's willing to be mulled over.
Into a stillness cleansed of all language
and scrubbed totally bare of psychology
objects of steam-soft consistency enter
with a cloud's propensity to wisp out of
shape, entrusting their tenuous integrity.
I have to be as breathless as a desert –
prickly pears and scorpions speckle
my emptiness, lowering their heartbeats
to critical levels; when all is said and done
I start writing in my mother's shorthand.

VISIBLY TOUCHED

Simply to be looked at is sufficient,
is exciting enough – to know her body's
privacies inspected; they tingle with self-
consciousness, and blush, rich in blood.
Renaissance theories of light and sight
had rays being emitted from the eyes –
the viewed object had to be caressed
by these protuberant lookings, snail-
horns going out with sensitive, shy,
wilting knobs to encounter the world.
But, more than that substantial gaze,
that tactile vision nudging her organs,
self-awareness is the spur of her arousal –
it is knowledge that most engorges her.

ADRENALIN

is the heart's petroleum, a boot-chemical
sent in to kick off cardiovascular recovery
without defibrillator paddles – the body's
accelerator, nudging it ahead or pressing
its pedal right down to the floorboards;
it's an evaporant hovering between spirit
and fire, an inflammable haze sequencing
explosions in ventricular burn chambers;
I am awash with it, soaked through, doused
in a virtually living fuel – a provocateur,
an inciter, incendiarist, a petrol bomber –
the body's necessary arsonist, setting alight
all those petulant sponges and muscles
moping in juices in the dark sullen torso.

EARTH-COLLAPSE

Over the ducking climbers passes
the angel of death, all two miles
of her – her wings of rock and ice;
she comes to a halt with her whole
weight resting on them, paralysed
from the neck down like a rubble
duvet, all of her musculature wasted
in avalanche – she has to be carted
away a bucketful at a time. Soon
she will relocate herself higher up
and shrug herself down into new
fields of unstable snow. Once dug up
the mountaineers will be found still
bent in their emergency crash positions.

THE DIFFERENCE

As rough as old Limpopo crocodiles
trees have surfaced to a new morning,
their leaves mottled with melanomas;
but they couldn't care less – complete
hair-loss after winter's chemotherapy
will leave them as indifferent as wood.
They're wonderful, but among the lower
orders of existence – even stick insects
have more nervous system than they do.
That summer's going to cure them of all
their ills won't give them any pleasure,
but we who have no bonus seasons
count every unrepeatable loss, and nerves
burn our feelings right into the skin.

BRIGHT STIPPLINGS

Sunlight as indiscriminate environment
pin-points thousands of individual
profferings of green; like the houselights
coming up, a general suffusion
enhances visibility everywhere at once
but still allows little catchments
of shine to be isolated on the very
outskirts of the trees, cupped in
precisely tailored botanical containers
where they sit like flames nurtured
by pores of oil; undifferentiating glow
has favoured them into prominence,
promoting their colours blunted only
by the soft materials they sparkle in.

FLUSHING OUT THE GAME

A light brush against your pubic hair
with the back of my fingers seemed
enough to start the antelope running
in your mind-savannah, a stampede
of carnal ungulates, of behaviours
well towards the other end of a scale
originating in your primly closed thighs.
The brazen disrespect of the gesture,
barely excused by its ambiguous
note of tenderness, introduced a whiff
of the satyr's bum, crude visions of rut
and erection; that first knuckle-brush
against your bush conceded, you were
quite happy to let the indecencies escalate.

WEATHER MASTERS

Who will wind the world-clock now,
now that the Attic deities have been
given short shrift like bogus sciences?
Who will dunk the sun into the sea?
We don't come across them anymore
winding sun-dials in a garden or being
naughty with their trousers around
their mucky hooves, the old flashers.
They have to be winkled intellectually
out of obscure books like oysters
shucked from their shells, tasting
not of the sea but of preserving salt.
They no longer strike the fear of god in us –
we're the ones who run the weather now.

SPIRALS

Sweet things are gathered into the poem,
tied together as it were by a flaxen ribbon,
like wrinkled seashells, driftwood, feathers,
tokens of the world at its most endearing,
iconic designs like spirals, arches, helixes
offering their suggestion of kindly intelligence;
this is a pastel nature rather than a red one;
both tooth and claw may figure, but only
as materials for necklaces, organic trinkets;
I can almost smell the lavender-scented
air-freshener in the gift shop that sells them;
far from what I take to be the real thing:
nature gulping nature in vortices of appetite,
stringy lumps being pulled apart by an owl.

THIS OBJECT

To semi-crawl into the warm ditch
for something glimpsed, in the already
rough and spent day, something that has
preserved the earliest blues of morning
in its four balanced parts, like extracted
irises of light vitrified in a square block
of glass; and just to examine this thing,
until the eyes grow tired, and noticing
starts to fade from them as leakage from
a porous material, and to come away with
certain measures of this object, imperfect
retentions of randomly recalled properties,
is about the best that can be done by way
of grateful tribute to this accidental world.

NAUGHTY GREENS

The rude vegetables are up to
no good again, succumbing
to irresistible inflations, their
growth-tips, tautly congested,
full of pregnant suggestion
and promise; mutating buds,
tinglingly alive with genetics,
obey (with slight infractions)
their guiding principle, bristle
with fresh implementations
of themselves; rooted in dung-
sweet earth, they reach their
swollen extensions up to my
window and give me the finger.

PERSUASION

Fishing with a text, the baited syntax
hooks complete assent from the reader;
the fly is feathered and fussed over,
the lure's charms are fixed to the barb;
whiplash suppleness and breaking strain
go hand in hand, leg muscles peruse
the velocities of the stream, brace,
clench and grip to keep the angler
standing; polish and lethal hazard
are as seductive as oysters sweating
like tongues in their crinkled shells;
as compelling as seasoning, taste buds
salt the rhetoric; flipped over, the mind
comes out still alive – whole, ganglial.

NATIVE LANGUAGE LANDSCAPE

Railway journeys clack through landscapes
inscrutable because of the languages spoken
in them – in hamlets, forges, dining rooms;
linguistic privilege permeates the animals
and trees, even the hills and wet polderlands
have a semantic advantage over me, making
the country seem unknowable, needing
translation; an irksome philological filter
between me and the rushing hedgerows
interrupts and troubles my looking – I must
burst through this film of native speaker
competence before I can fully observe –
farms, ditches, windmills and cows hidden
from view behind Dutch and Danish names.

TRUMPET RASPBERRY

A trumpet's long cylinder
is folded back upon itself
just like the human gut into
a compact manifold of coils.
All the way from its mouth,
belled wide open to make
the crassest and brashest noises
in the orchestra, the trumpet's
brass intestines extend through
sinuous bends to its pouting
rectum where the trumpeter
has applied his own pursed lips
and blows a loud musical fart
up the body of the instrument.

SPRING EPIDEMIOLOGY

The branches are waving their sores
in a fresh, trunk-torquing wind.
Like a simultaneous rash, red
lesions have appeared all over
the tree, budding tumours putting
out their first inflammations.
Coloured like mouldy green metal
branches bend within a rosy
mist of infection, as beautiful as
cancer cells or a bank of pink coral.
The epidemic has jumped trees,
diseasing a whole tranche of time;
a low-temperature fever has lit
the trees with flowery tuberculosis.

TARMAC AND TAPESTRY

On one side, the smelly road-spewer, caked
with tar and bitumen, clanking with stones
and clunky engineering, oozes out a burnt
strip of highway, as deep and hot as a roly
poly of volcanic lava; it stings like boiling jam
and reeks of black materials smoking from
the oven; all is industrial coal and creosote.
As if straight off a webbed and shuttling
loom roll unicorns, cavalry officers, kings
and their banqueting halls, where everything
is chronicled in a warp and woof of linen.
How silently the looms of language sound
their hunting horns in the mind's emptiness.

SONNET HORNET

My old peg-leg pirouettes,
exudes her language pigment,
hops from word to word,
drains the fluid from her
long slim storage tank,
spins ink into orthography;
somewhere above the spindle
spooling its lexical drool
a volume of memory hovers
as roomy as an empty suitcase;
she draws its blackness
into her burning needle
and annotates the emptiness
with discharges of octopus ink.

A FOOD AMNESTY

Something as tangy as coal tar
lands in an unprepared mouth:
buds at the back of the tongue
go into shock when fishy brews
of oceanic astringency invade
inexperienced pores; such jolts
by freak off-the-scale flavours
can traumatise that organ for life;
ripples of disgust will wrinkle it
like salt shrimping a wet snail;
but one day you may let those nasty
flavours back into your mouth,
extending a gastric amnesty to
avocado, beetroot, crabmeat and gin.

MY PENITENTIAL GREENS

Bitter salad sloshed with doctored oil
will furnish the green moral context
of my salmon – a short life fished out
of a sea-farm where freedom was faked
a few nylon barriers away from the bare
powers of the uncurtailed Atlantic, with
just enough wide water to encourage
layers of sweet, melting fish product
onto fine feathery bones; sour lettuce
and stalky rocket serve as my apology
to all the creatures I insult by eating –
even so I must ease with oil and garlic
these prickly nests that beset my mouth
like tangles of grasshopper legs and wings.

STEEPED IN WORLD

The mountain sweats
sweet mineral streams,
trickles clean orange
water through matted
furze, penetrating
rough stalk flesh to
inner marrowbone;
seep your mind into
roots and rocks until
it owns the material,
injects its language
into bud and stone,
lights noun-lamps
in wasp and restio.

THE POLITICS OF A DUTIFUL DAUGHTER

She tells us the talks are starting to bear fruit
but what exactly is her definition of fruit?
Are they what we might call tripe and onions?
For too long she's been feeding us her gospel
of this-will-be-good-for-you, victuals straight
off the vicar's table, a bland Protestant diet
garnished with orthodox Presbyterian greens –
mealtimes of napkins and piety, headaches
and secret shame. Late at night she would pass
her father's study and hear God and the vicar
locked in loud, rancorous argument, both
quoting from Heidegger to prove their point.
One day the vicar emerged victorious. Jehovah
stormed off and vented his fury over Phuket.

IN HIS OWN IMAGE

God wriggles into the full human
body-suit, pushes himself hard
into the very ends of his feet,
pulls his hands on tight,
slips into his liver, permeates
fat reserves with his divinity,
then turns all the vital motors on
and passes control to the brain.
Now all he has to do is wait – for
the growth of fingernails, hunger
pangs, the first calls of nature;
and that weird sensation of having to use
simple muscle contractions
in place of his old omnipotence.

EYEBALLED BY AN ANT

Like cysts or styes plugged into
our human flesh, our daily rooms
are strewn with hidden insects;
sprinkled inside wood and plaster
these minimal flecks of life dot
our domestic interiors; like pustules
and verrucas they try us, force us
into defensive philosophy – mites
so intimately and eponymously
accommodated challenge belief
in our ascendancy; every now
and again one ventures out on six
or eight legs and boldly eyes us –
we quail at its tiny, insolent stare.

ENNUI

The machinery of delight
was running its motors
deliriously in small groups
of daffodils whose blossoms
were transfigured by sunlight
into flakes of buttery gold;
but I took no joy in them –
puissance and *jouissance*
blazed in the petal dresses
but the little margarine-
coloured flowers shone
in vain – their yellows
on full beam in the face
of my indifference to them.

DESCRIPTIVE LIMITS

That shine is indescribable, the way
it overturns the morning gloom
by filling leaves with lived-in light
assisted by the chemicals of autumn;
this radiance arrives with a powerful
note of departure – something divine
has gone, leaving golden scrapings
in the trees, a burning residue that is
the aftermath of earlier possession;
to hold a deposit so sharp and clean
those receptacles would have to be
incapable of feeling, and yet they seem
to share our delight – as if that shining
is how they show us their amazement.

SLEEPING SWANS

You came upon a family of sleeping swans –
the mother with her sons and daughters
all wrapped together on a weave of marsh
grasses, necks and bodies lightly embracing.
A decision of surrender has left them warm,
bundled together in chosen unconsciousness.
An absence as much as a presence, a choice
to be as vulnerable as orchids growing wild,
they repose their downy anatomies, drawing
into delicate lungs air scented by lake water
and ferns through small nostril-punctures
in their horny beaks. Their swan-songs muted
to the soft drone of sleep, they lie like a heap
of Scottish bagpipes the pipers have lain aside.

FLIGHT READINESS

The seeds are drying out their wings,
getting ready to fly. All the knotty power
of the tree, all that hydraulic strength
humming up through the sap-wires
in its backbones to its frilliest edgings –
all for the sake of these small brown discs.
Packed like hampers with complete dinners
including knives and forks, napkins,
wine glasses and apple pie, the seeds
have everything on board, but only one
in ten thousand will lay out its biology
in a full-scale picnic. No matter –
they're all eager to spin dizzyingly into
the firmament like tiny replicas of Saturn.

BRAIN HABITAT

I have to be kept behind thick glass,
hermetically molly-coddled, regulated
by thermostats, held at arm's length
from upsetting weather – for I am
a human, i.e. a protected species.
I cannot be placed in direct contact
with low temperatures, rough air,
dripping trees; hard knocks like that
would be the death of me; even sparrows
are tougher, in touch with the orders
of nature *al dente*; that's why I seek out
the forgiving haven of inside my head –
that's the only place I can be myself,
take all my clothes off and be naked.

JOHN RUSKIN, *Blenheim Orange Apple*

An intent look assisted
by reading glasses slides
over the sweeps of the apple,
falls into unison with
its curved gravities;
memories of apple pigment
and polished waxes of skin
cling to the travelling eye;
now the eye uncovers
a smell: century-old paint
giving off apple-whiff;
passed from sense to sense
the apple weighs, has bite,
is crisp, contemporaneous.

SEASONAL EUPHORIA

A shrub is shaking its amber flowers
whose beams of light are quenched
in the very blossoms that shine them.
The wind's role in this may be inferred
from the agitations that grip the plant.
Like a stallion tossing its thick mane
the bush is whipping the long necks
of its branches, drawing attention to
the small floral heads that crest them
like coloured mantises clinging firmly
with their hooked feet and thorny legs.
A new bout of springtime is pending
and the bush seems jubilant about this,
putting out buds and bursting them orange.

CROWS CLOWNING IN THE AIR

We catch them at their very best,
a best so good it allows them
to hurl their bodies recklessly into
a momentary collapse of form
before recovering themselves
mid-air, with a wrench of effort;
they stall, fall into crumpled balls
of carbon feathers, then with a deep
scoop of wings, regain their glide.
So athletic they are, so expended,
we forget that, weeks from now,
they will be shoved pitifully under
hedges to die, in an act of disposal
so all-pervasive we barely notice it.

EXACTLY TEN O'CLOCK

The clock full of pre-determined metal
has been sprung like a poacher's iron trap.
Uncoiling the latencies of its potential
in mechanical energy, it releases itself
tooth by tooth like a river flowing
with lessening force to the annulling lake.
It beats out its temporal messages
heedlessly, as much unconcerned about
planetary transits and orbits as about
appointments with your chiropodist
or fitting in a trip to the butcher's shop
before the post office closes; no hungers
or urgencies propel it to greater haste
or influence its dark Newtonian tread.

SNAP

We set the trap, pressing a cube
of old cheddar onto the spike
at the prow of the "little snapper"
attested by countless victims;
the wire walloper is pulled back
against a stiffly coiled spring,
the trigger-arm folded across
and tucked under a steel lip
on the pressure-plate – this will
receive the weight of the mouse,
that feart and jittery beast
whose footfall on this delicate
set-up will unleash the ferocity
of all that invisibly pent-up steel.

A GLASS SONNET

The poem-blower exhales into
his chosen forms, the empty grids
of quatrain, sonnet, villanelle;

his words fill up its chambers
one segment at a time, bulkheads
in the smooth hull of the poem;

he blows English, or some other
language, into the sounding body
of his vessel, flooding its glass-

bottomed shape with air to keep
it buoyant in the cold linguistic
ocean it floats upon, a breath

to keep it riding over the world –
kelp, octopus, ray, pink shellfish.

FIT AS A FLY

The physics of being a successful animal
is the house-fly's physiological adaptation
to pure panes of glass; pin-claws used
for scrambling on bark; a tree-ape's
smooth equipoise, its gyroscopic glide
mounting to an ecliptic of perfect balance;
such powers have deserted the likes of me
whose contact with surfaces is limited
to the soles of my feet; except that
I clamber primate-like through acts
of love, relishing opportunities for
satisfying frictions of purchase and grip;
as the magnetic fly adheres to glass
mirroring grasps cleave me to my love.

BEEF CHEEKS AND CAULIFLOWER

Roasting a whole head of cauliflower intact
is like cooking the brains of this vegetable;
it too has a hard cortical stem leading from
the lobes to a thick, truncheon-like body;
all of this spongy stuff, though white and tasteless,
is edible if soaked in garlicky, mustardy juices;
the consuming of it is untroubled by dreams
that couldn't be washed out of the grey matter;
but eating beef cheeks is a bit close to the bone,
isn't it – cheeks are adjacent to the personality;
we'll be gutting the head to cook that next,
and finding it rather chewy and opinionated;
cuts of cow-mentality will stop our mouths
with cognitive stew – sinewy, full of attitude.

SECEDING EMBODIMENT

Their equivalent of an ear
allows the dead to hear
our praises; some travesty
of blood allows blushes
of modesty; in quintillions
of eternities from now those
wisps of ontology will still
be recalling their 80 summers
of embodiment; confined to
the absolute sterility of
their afterlife, what nostalgia
for the years when they
could still smell the sweet
putrefactions of autumn.

SHATTERPROOF

A dark sound from the Corvid family
crashes right through the plate glass
without causing it any damage (something
to do with physics) – the glass might as well
not be there, so clearly and completely
does the voice of the bird crack through it;
its cry is as bright as chisels, or as soft
as liquorice – authentic Crow, perfectly
understandable despite its passage into
and out of the glass – the glass unchanged,
as if it just opened up to let the sound in,
then closed again, like water – nothing
shattered, even though that anarchic cry
was hurled through the window like a brick.

ICE

Cobras of slithery panic lie coiled
around my heart. Fear slides me
out of sleep into their contractions.
Like Medusa's head my heart shakes
its serpents, the aortas drinking
from its ventricles, red- and blue-
barred watersnakes that go in and out
of its reluctant chambers, feeding off
muscle twitch and squirts of blood.
The world enters me like drip-lines,
dissolving salt, adrenalin and dread
into the coronary vessels, speeding
along to dart their ice-needles into
my flapping and floundering heart.

ALBUMINOUS SQUID

In the squid's body is a bone
shaped like a gull's feather,
a stiff white quill floating
freely in the transparent ink
of the animal's abdomen –
a creature less fish than small
underwater calligraphy kit
for writing invisible poems.
The fishmonger is cleaning
its blond and boneless body,
the white frond stiffening it;
black ink spurts – he yelps
a curse – his apron sprinkled
with unintelligible verse.

ON MY LATE ESPOUSED SAINT

I woke up this morning married to Barbara.
This was something she had often requested,
pointing reproachfully at her ringless finger.
The marriage didn't last long, as could have been
predicted – it was all over in a minute – a tender
dream had performed the nuptials in my sleep,
had popped the question and won her consent.
In gratitude I'd slid my arms around her waist
which was swollen and puffy an account of
her anti-depressant medication, but my affection
for her was undiminished – unfeigned and fond.
The difficulty this espousal posed for my current
way of life was just beginning to dawn on me
when dawn itself arrived and annulled the union.

POWER

An avalanche the size of
a small provincial town
whispers down the valley,
altering significant geography
in minutes; the mountain
can't hold itself upright,
its weight is beyond itself,
beyond all the cohesions
of limestone and pegmatite;
more stupendous forces
are sapping the iron out of
its ores; they want that proud
white summit brought low
for the grazing of sheep.

TRANNY

Female ghost in a masculine machine –
not all the sex medicines on the market
can go far enough to reverse the damage;
the most advanced Ovidian drugs cannot
carry her conversion to full womanhood;
something of the ousted male remains,
something stubbornly chromosomal
that persists in the mannish jaw, unripe
hips, the general muggishness of the phiz;
the hormonal gravel that gathered in her
during adolescence will never soften inside
her vocal tract; for that she would need
the help of cynical gods – those very ones
who cocked her body up in the first place.

WOMAN RECLINING ON A LEOPARD SKIN
(Otto Dix, 1927)

Her body curled about its second
sex invites with viperish coils
aficionados of libidinous venom;
elastic garters grip satisfying thighs;
a virus housed in the oyster
would prostrate more delicate men
but robuster appetites can thole it;
she is ferocious and professional;
her spine has a python's languorous
twist from neck to tail; she is Berlin;
she is putsch and poverty, *kultur-*
shock and cliteromania; find her,
you pale and unassuming cameras;
experience her and get over her.

THE VAGINA

Her magnificent hollow organ
has folds of skin thrown up
onto the surface like the earth
sprayed from a mole's burrow,
or curly shavings of wood left
under a lathe, or tresses of water
that are formed when a stream
is interrupted by a stick; from
chamber to chamber it leads
like a cave system to regions
mysterious even to its owner,
where, far from inhabited places,
strange privy councils hold court
and rule with imperious laws.

WELL-EARNED GROWTH RINGS

I trust the intelligence of the tree;
it's more than just a pretty face;
it sprinkles exactly the right number
of pink rattles throughout its domain,
its fabric heartily shagged with parasites
– from wasp lumps to tough bacteria –
encouraging century-long immunities;
some of its brilliant floral improvs
may well be sitting spurned, washed up
and out on a limb; it may even end its days
as a provider of wooden laundry pegs,
but right now how confidently
this handsome machine of thought thinks
the long-brooded concepts of biology.

EATING SQUID

Lying on the fishmonger's tray
is a body like a piece of offal —
slimy white viscera or section
of the small intestine of a sheep.
It's like the working part of some
bigger animal, an extracted throat
or gullet, a vocal tract which is all
sinew and tendon, a utilitarian bit
too gristly to eat. Its price reflects
the mundane and ugly nature of
the beast itself. This albino tube
may suggest an absence of taste
but careful grilling will release
a subtle sweetness of sea animal.

ACID RECALL

If I had lived my life mathematically,
calculating my decisions with compasses,
protractors and sharpened pencils,
instead of having lived it with guts
and gore, by the red lamp of psychiatry,
I might have spared myself and others
the malfeasance of rushed or purposeless
choices motivated by the large intestines
or more precisely by the contents thereof.
What the hell was I thinking? Now I yelp
whenever a stingingly naff choice of mine
gushes unforgivingly to mind, forcing me
to own up to my visceral inadequacies
with a resurgence as searing as acid reflux.

DAVID HOCKNEY'S ARRIVAL OF SPRING

Hockney arrives to measure the bud-
knobbled beginnings of a black and white
spring – charcoal whispering on cartridge
paper carries rut puddles and reflections,
damp days, sunlight glowing in rural lanes
onto the stiff white medium, coaxed
into representation, his optical illusions
infused with ecstatic ontological veracity;
fleeting vegetation is grabbed by its after-
images, in the very act of its departure,
and that elated impression of its brief
stay is mimicked in charcoal, annotated
by fugitive dustings as blurry as old eyes,
by incisions as penetrating as slug or sloe.

A PRAGMATIC CROW

A crow on concrete who briefly
stopped to eat the water lying there
angled the dark pip of his eye
and found our human agitations
behind plate glass too ambiguous
to bear, so humped himself into space
and beat blackness into solid air
and slid across to a deep green tree;
may he there find the wild peace
our rectilinear architecture denies him,
though he won't find in its boughs
ledges of remnant rain, flats of wet
tainted by the rust of savoury iron
and flushed with industrial flavours.

AN INSECT OF THE ORDER ODONATA

That glitzy dragonfly reposing on a lily pad
is as lean and voracious as a 6-inch nail;
it has failed to ripen into its full Linnean order,
as one of its 4 helicopter wings is part missing.
But that doesn't impair its hunting capacity –
its rapacity originates in the nymph stage, when
it will eat anything full of genetic promise.
Nature has prepared thousands of tasty little
fairy princesses for it to devour, swallowing
them whole – ball gowns, slippers, tiaras and all –
not omitting the eyes and small capable brains.
Sympathy is running high, however, for this
maimed insect – a tie-pin with the whole world
of summer scattered across its diamantine eye.

LOCK UP YOUR DRAWERS

A fistful of crumpled black cotton
peeled off her body and tossed onto
the floor has aroused my suspicions;
I drop to all fours to investigate –
I become a dog, my sense of smell
elevated; I lift and trickle the fabric
through my fingers like an epicure
admiring the cool, clicking masses
of a necklace – lustrous black pearls
as slippery as silicone; white soiling
on the padded gusset is confirmed;
but a near-sacramental elevation
to the nostrils finds no incriminating
odours – I leave myself unmolested.

CLOSE TO PERFECTION

A lightweight fly hobbling
over hairs on a plant's leg
is in its domain, awkward
though its insect passage be;
a mite in the waxy canyons
of a flower's ear edges around
something green and hindering;
both are at their apex – newly
machined from nothingness,
they are complete packages
of neurology working their way
into pure, sweet manna, sucking
it up with the tiny dissolving
irritations of their mouth parts.

A SOLO WEDDING IN KYOTO

The self-pleasurer has granted herself
permission to take full responsibility
for all of her own sexual gratification.
After consulting her spiritual mentors,
she has given her preferred practices
the green light, and is good to go.
She puts herself under the spell of her
preparations like one of those virgins
who marries herself in a solo wedding
in Kyoto – soft lights, heaped pillows,
vibrators, oils, cucumbers, butt-plugs
and scented candles; she rings herself,
vows fealty, and consummates the union
by frigging herself until daybreak.

STIFF AND SALTY BOOTS
on the poetry of George Mackay Brown

Sea seeps onto his pages; salt water,
stilled from frantic mid-ocean, soaks
into his craft, twists island phonetics
into coastal images and sea business;
mist wets the wiring of the grammar,
dampening hinges of syntax; fleets sail
into his engulfing clauses, crab claws
and three-dimensional dancing boots
stand in full, round, sturdy cobblery;
soggy oranges litter the coastline
where ships broke; later, sea-fattened
sailors arrive, face-down; villagers
will hook them in, still learning how
to square the bounty with the horror.

STAR TRAVELLER

Negotiating essential things
with our haphazard array
of capabilities and instruments
we're either a comical anomaly
in the expressionless cosmos,
a bit of evolution that over-
cooked itself, going beyond
pragmatism to self-awareness,
or else we're existential heroes
racking our logic boxes
to try and solve the galaxies;
this forager, this fornicator,
looks up and shields his star-directed eyes
with five practical fingers.

TALES FROM PLUTARCH

Hogs will eat river crabs
to cure a headache
Plutarch assures us.
They will dig these
delicacies up out of
soft riverbank mud
whenever their heads
thump with a migraine.
As they normally eat
rotten shite, scoffing
succulent crab meat
must be a real gourmet
treat to a pig. And what
better way of telling
they've got a sore head?

MOTHER AND DAUGHTER

She can reveal all of her distress to you;
she trusts you enough to unmask herself
as ugly, weak, defenceless and distraught;
her screwed-up face, awash with tears,
is twisted like a spoon bent by Uri Geller;
it hoots all the howled words of lament;
self-pity thumps up from her diaphragm
in jerky jazz rhythms like a double bass;
there is no shame in the swimming eyes,
no sting at all in the salt of her weeping;
the sorrow comes up whole like a wreck
lifted, seas pouring off its surfaced decks,
a drowned ship beautiful in its salvage,
rigged & polished, its timbers stoven in.

SOFT ENOUGH TO EAT

Most living things have a chewy
consistency which meat-crazy birds
take advantage of with hornlike
bill-hooks muffled in their down;
you can grip such gummy matter
and wrench pieces off it with a good
twist; the black eyes of owls trap
the tiniest fragments of light, eyes
like inky marble or like glassy ink.
Owls fly very silently, with approximately
point zero zero something decibels
of noise; but when they make contact
it's the chewability, the easy avulsion
of small animals that they feast upon.

WINGED AND WONDERFUL

Dinkum fairies – coupla inches
tall, rattling wings, sweet natures –
abound, as orders of the Acrididae;
always ready to transmogrify from
Nile mud at a nod from thunder,
no shortage of reserve battalions
in the endless war of the species;
they rose to perfection early on
and stopped just there; they, if any,
will escape destruction's sufficing
fire and ice; but then they'll sweep
the world in vain for wheat to strip
or human turds to lay their eggs in.

PALLIATIVES FOR A TORMENTED PARLIAMENT

Let us reason without rhetoric,
use arguments as pure as honey,
without additives, clean and sweet,
so limpid and free of impurities
you could spot the flimsiest flaw
of metaphor, of false persuasion,
if you held it up to the light;
let our logic be water, straight
from the tap, colourless, lucid,
without mineral taint, filtered
through sieves of Aristotelian
syllogism; let no rank odours
of flowery imposition wrinkle
our noses or pucker our brows.

TIME'S NUMBERING CLOCK

Time ticked with bees and hollyhocks;
the world became time's matter-clock;
flies buzzed themselves to a standstill;
flowers drank vases empty and marked
their passing with corruption in the petals;
migrating flocks flying asleep on the wing
melted a hundred longitudes into none
and crossed them in the blink of an eye;
whole oceans sang themselves dry, sinking
down through salinations and sounds.
I was a fire-clock, burning full minutes
of my own sugars, fats and energy stores;
even plastics and nuclear waste weren't spared
but hearts and galaxies bore the brunt of it.

READERS OF GOD

Heroes of exactness and measurement
spend their lives reading clock faces
and thermometers, consulting pressure
gauges, tapping their temperature dials
and noting down articulate numbers.
They are masters of secondary evidence,
of the wires, currents and amp meters
mediating the immaculate, immeasurable
essence, perhaps divine, of the elements.
A flinch in the instrument, a needle's qualm,
gives a sign, from deep in the infinitely
regressed heart of matter, that an absent
Creator is still at work, trying to make good
the design blunders of his wobbly universe.

A TALE FROM OVID

Actaeon's eye caught the eye of a dog
as it buried its fangs in his face; that look
will last longer in the mind of the dog
than the ripped-off cheek that passes
through the body of the dog – chewed,
dismantled by enzymes, then shat out;
that haunting glance will roll around
its skull like a glass eye irised with blue;
it will keep inspecting him from within,
casting its hooded look at him balefully,
forming part of the dog's introspection,
adding its soul to the soul of the dog;
harder than gristle or button or bone
is that final blue rebuke from its master.

SEEING QUINCE

Leaves like citrus peels
embitter the autumn trees;
their colours go for
our stomachs, setting off
a release of gastric juices —
our eyes carry into
our mouths a taste of
lemon curd and lime jelly;
some early embryonic
mix-up of optic nerve
and salivary gland
makes the gingering season
appeal to our tongues
as sour confectionary.

PLAYING WITH MY CHRISTIANITY

Sometimes I unpack my childhood religion
and play with its Roman soldiers, prostitutes
and moneylenders, its demons, Archangels
and cardboard Nativity scenes, its donkeys,
Herods, and its angry God – all the props
that make it so charming and antiquated.
Its strict little universe dances around me
like a brass orrery of squealing satellites –
unoiled celestial bodies circling the earth
at its centre; in the end, both its believers
and its nonbelievers are allocated to their
well-deserved eternities, and I pack away
my little model of Christianity, so very glad
that the actual world in no way resembles it.

CONCRETE DIPPING BASIN

When the tide drew back for a better
look at us, a concrete tidal trough was
left behind – filled to the brim
with clear new water, a fresh scoop
from the sea, so clean that it was
invisible, and cold as the Atlantic.
Small organic particles of the ocean
sparkled in the salty crystal brine.
We sank down into it, drawing
swirls of clammy seaweed around
our nakedness. Responding to your
nipples tightening with goose bumps,
I gave myself leave to poke a head
of white asparagus above the green.

SOUND-CREEP

When noise travels, air's not its only option.
It can sidle along walls like a secret agent,
can mumble inside the walls themselves,
creeping disease-like through the fabric.
It can hook itself into brickwork and timber,
infiltrate the mains water system, embody
itself in the knots and grains of floorboards.
This multiplicity of indirect voyaging means
that the midnight sufferer cannot tell where
the party is coming from – upstairs, downstairs,
right next door or several tenements away.
All he knows is that the revelry has traversed
many materials to get to him, and has now
taken hold of him by the bones of his ears.

YEAH! YEAH! YEAH!

Like the layer of black deposit
left by a volcano, the Fab Four
ran a seam of epoch-making ore
through all our lives, crossing
from one continent to the next,
leaving its smudgy rim of ash
or sediment in nearly every life
on the planet; scientists sifting,
weighing and carbon-dating us
years hence will find, chalked
in our genetic bar-codes, signs
of that event – that ecstatic leap
into song, that sudden yelp
of elation in the seismic chart.

THE FLY IS A PERFECT EXAMPLE

As light as a breadcrumb
but vastly more intricate,
it has a small-scale version
of the will, just enough
for changes of direction
to avoid being swatted;
a lot of concentration,
(a watchmaker's, through
thick magnifying glass)
must have gone into
the making of its feet;
the workmanship there
and elsewhere would put
a Russian silversmith to shame.

COUNTRY PROVERBS

A stream squeezes around
the calves of Heraclitus;
a fish in the same stream
fins monotonously
to stay motionless *vis-à-vis*
a calf standing on the bank;
the stream washes the gills
of the fish, excites oxygen-
extracting hairs that nip
the O's off all the H_2O's;
fishermen at night carry
oil and canvas lanterns
to the river; mellow beams
butter up the finning fish.

AARGH!

The little brains of the crows
are agitated, making them try
to say a thousand things
with the same short ugly outburst;
they must be gutted not to have
transformational grammar
at their disposal on such occasions.
Dressed up like church elders
at a Scottish synod, they can't cry
'Bloody Hell!' when they get all
worked up about the situation.
Without more of that Chomskian
stuff in their heads these poor
animals can't even swear properly.

ON THE TRAIN TO FISH HOEK

Far more distracting than a whole landscape
is her face – its blend of goodness and beauty
abashes the intruding eye. The pleasure
it affords or denies raises the onlooker's
guilty discomfort to eye-lowering levels.
The look is an infringement, tolerated
only in the smallest sips of observation;
prolonged, it is a rape. I once subjected
a fellow rail-traveller to twenty minutes
of sustained visual attack, a brutally unchecked
scrutiny of everything her face had to offer
and was not given the choice of withholding.
That same suburban line is a horror nowadays –
crawling with gangsters, rapists and muggers.

LEAFING CREEPER

Something wonderful is crawling up my
window – the sprouting explorer-shoot
of a creeper, as vulnerable as tumescence.
It nods its erection against the glass,
its glans a bud that will throw leaves
to the left and to the right as it bursts;
the bud is already split like a cleft palate –
it would lisp if it could speak, but it's
deaf and dumb, all its needs are satisfied
by mimings of botanical necessity;
it stiffens as it grows, it is a sexual being –
its growth nudges it askance at regular
intervals, producing kinks in the shaft;
but the soft, seeking tip feels not a thing.

OUT OF THE FORCING-BOX

Three weeks in the incubator
forced me onto the discipline
of self-pleasuring; I was already
far gone in onanism and solipsism
when the box was opened
and I was let out into humanity;
friendship remained an enigma,
the why no less than the how;
sex was the only compromise –
to form a continuous bridge
of tissue so that I might pull
myself organ after organ into
the precinct of another person
like a double-yoked mutation.

WILKINSON SWORD

Inhabit the instrument, sentence:
a bamboo-handled razor will do;
give it shoulders and elbows
and a screw to open the wings
of the blade-housing unit;
let it repose wrapped in linen
inside the shaving box Napoleon
took to the Battle of Austerlitz;
let it rasp over the isobars
of his sturdy Corsican chin;
become the warmth of bamboo,
become steel and ivory inlay,
open and shut your hinges, grip
the Gilette blade and bite down.

DEAD MUSICAL TREES

Trees were just left to die where they stood
in Bechuanaland – their sucking-systems
finding less and less to draw up; some, dead on
their feet for years, revived to mock us; others,
like Rilke's Eurydice, were far too snuffed out
to be called back from where they'd gone to;
their very natures had shifted within the Table
of Elements, from the botanical to something
almost metallic – an aluminium facsimile
dulled to its last mineral glimmer; and then
like sad, stiff violinists, they would scratch out
works of high-friction, barbed-wire orchestras,
harsh songs squealed from thorny instruments,
the creaking windmill music of a rusty Orpheus.

TRANSMISSION

All the horrors run safely in the box:
blood, warfare and assault are carried
inside valves, diodes and tuning coils,
containment-materials that soak up
and shield us from the catastrophic
world – bloody coups flow along
copper wires, galaxies burn their
infinite fuels inside vacuum tubes;
in spaces thin as the Queen of Hearts
women are punched, flats collapse,
floods corner families in their cellars;
but when we try to switch them off
we carry those theatres of war to bed
inside the Trojan horses of our heads.

FORCES ON PHRASAL TEXTURE

A telling formulation dissolves in
a solution of sodium forgetfulness,
its proteins and peptides dismantled
into units of purest micro-biology.
Enamel erosion of its consonants
leaves crescents of nail clippings,
a shingly residue of teeth, gall-stones;
enzymes and other strippers eat away
at nouns and soft connecting words.
Air-shifts pull clauses apart, thinning
the body, unsubstantiating it, undoing it
as a substrate for sense and reference;
it's gone now, grope as you will, up to
your elbows in wisps of foggy dispersal.

ATROPHY AND REGENERATION

Half the body snores
in superannuation,
its muscles liquified
and drained away;
ambition cannot
spread to that half
unless we regrow
threads in the water,
preparatory pathways
to carry the materials
for fresh bone to knit,
plaiting moral fibres
where new skills may
root and revolutionise.

CROW LANDING

Angular as a swastika the crow lands,
crooking its elbows, legs thrust ahead.
Body and wings draw themselves up
like a bent penknife to await the crash.
Branches melt backwards into the springs
of their sway, air-bagging the shock.
The flight breaks up, sprouts chaotic
claws and feathers which stick ungainly
paddles out of earlier elegant soaring.
A thousand corrections to rudders, flaps
and ailerons bring the bird convincingly
to perch. Its weight tips forward like
a curling wave; wings retract; the crow
stills itself to a vigilant, black blossom.

TALKIN' 'BOUT MY GENERATION

Desire ages just as the body ages,
keeps in step with it – older eyes
demand flawed teeth, duller skin;
heavy usage and healed injuries
(inebriation, hurts of motherhood,
and sex) have stretched her, not out of
but into shape – more than six decades
boast of their unopposed sway;
but all that my gaze finds here now
is so sweet to contemplate, a meet
rejoinder to my own advanced years;
matching abrasions have scarred us
in parallel; her complementary decay
is what makes her so fresh in my eyes.

PERFORMATIVE UTTERANCE
How to Do Things with Words

Language may lick where the tongue
is disallowed – a lingual ambassador
given leave to enter the locked Russia
of another's life, words doing the work
of the hands and the insinuating voice;
phrases practice their surrogacy, load
themselves with as much colour, pollen
and suggestion as they can carry, and rub
these into the perusing mind; criminal
acts of vocalisation smuggle a delicious
contraband of silk, vodka and poetry sewn
into the grunted underwiring of glottals;
they give us the scratch of her suspenders,
the very crackle of her nylons, so to speak.

ENGINE PHILOLOGY

Get your head into the tubing
of language, its oesophagus
and ventilation pipes, the works
and combustion-engine design
of the thing; stick your head
under the chassis and fiddle
with sumps and pistons, drive-
shafts and fan-belts that make
up all the dirty machinery of it.
Unscrew the mechanics of
negation, follow the wiring to
auxiliary and ignition systems
where gearbox and voicebox
fuse a single humachine being.

WRITING FOR THE MOUTH

Sweeten your lines with watermelon,
gladden your sticky-fingered readers
with dried figs and powdery delights;
they're a sensual lot, eager for sensory
knock-about and trauma in your language;
don't disappoint them, blow strong
smells throughout your verse, bad ones
too – they can't give offence, they're only
linguistic; splash childish colours around,
big tigerish reds and tart primary greens
(pastels would just get diluted in vowels);
words are snail-shaped objects to be held
on the tongue before the reader bites down
to taste the bitter effusions of semantics.

NOT SUCH A PATHETIC FALLACY

Gone suddenly pink, the morning sky
has tinted itself without the expedient
of oil paint or blood; its remote (and
illusory) membrane is an epitome
of indifference, of what will carry on
freezing and flushing mechanically
long after the human innings is over;
imputing sentimentalities and organs
to it is a well-known lure of derision;
but no – nothing is without anthropo-
morphic meddling; I'm viewing it all
through thick layers of my own body;
everywhere I see only myself, already
out there the instant I open my eyes.

LESSONS IN BAROQUE DECORUM

To the immense relief of all classical music
I lowered my cheap Yamaha from the Bach
Flute Sonata whose sacred joy I was mocking
with sacrilegious misfingerings; and fell silent.
That's when you launched your tirade, Wenger.
Whatever it was crushing for a teacher to say
to his pupil you said. In your rage you swung
your own flute, a thousand thalers of aristocratic
craftsmanship from Bonn, and clipped the stand.
The mere dimple of damage left on its cylinder
was equivalent to a heart attack in the instrument —
that little dint knocked all the harmonic advantages
of decades of disciplined and beautiful playing
into a jangle of iron filings. Earth felt the wound.

THE LOCUST DAUGHTERS

The daughters return home and place
their broken bodies on the cold ground;
the world has given them a beating –
colleagues, lovers, sous-chefs and siblings
have all had a go at them; their wombs
have neither excused nor exempted them
as they might have hoped; now they are
brawl- and battle-mauled; all they own
are plastic bags stuffed with dirty washing
they salvaged from a previous address;
here they will lie until their skins heal
and harden and their bite comes back;
from these pupae brand new daughters
will hatch, even more terrifying than the old.

AGES OF APOGEES

The sun keeps rising and setting over
her body – I have seen some comings
and goings over her years; her mind
is a forced occupation, suffering
successions of control, enthusiasms
laying yokes of terror on her shoulders;
her body is tidal, sometimes pulling
back to show spine or rib protrusions,
sometimes flooding her to the neck,
pushing the tidal fat into every bay
and inlet of her figure; summers
and autumns draped her in scented
linens; she is ageing like a planet
celebrating its birthdays in icy orbits.

SPELT

A hairy, rug-like texture in the food
does wonders for your slick insides;
every mouthful honours the environment;
the landscape heals visibly, its skin
blemishes clearing up with each swallow;
you can eat yourself good, your moral
nature predicated on a dogma of diet,
your recipes followed like gospel texts;
a pharmacy of grasses grows wild
outside your front door, clipped down
by clinics of self-medicating animals;
but especially those long gut-passages,
stuffed into the body's hollows, thrive
on little ecologies of saintly enzymes.

LESSONS FROM A NATIVE

A native reconciles me
to glass-like slivers of fish
unsettling the lucidity of water
in a whimpering stream
rubbing its way forwards
with the lightest of touches.
The water leaves promptly,
exiting into weed-thickets;
the fishes are left behind
like small optical flaws
in the vision of the water.
The native allows me to share
(with borrowed nationality)
all of these alien materials.

LOVE AMONG THE OVER-SIXTIES

Her body is full of unseen flaws
waiting to flourish in later life –
some propensities of the spine
that will twist her like a harp,
a faint prophetic flush of dyes
under the skin that will become
discoloured, hard and nodular
over time, concealed by creams.
Her psychology also will turn
more bitter and concentrated,
losing its winning ameliorations,
foregrounding its harsher,
underlying tannins. And at just
that time we ourselves will lose
our childish fear of imperfections.

AN AMBIVALENT BEQUEST

Part endowment, part liability,
part life-craft, part curse, her body
rolls beneath her, rocking smoothly
on its pivots of cushioned bone;
pride and despair alternate with
every step at this resented ownership;
less visible to her than to her lover,
less easy to inspect by eye or finger,
that infuriating draughtsmanship
of ball and socket, calf and septum
convinces her she was dealt a bummer;
but any casual onlooker, demurring,
would run over her buttery motions
the blasphemous idolatry of his eyes.

BULAWAYO SEX LESSONS

Hibiscus flowers were ballerinas
on point, in stiff taffeta tutus.
We undressed them, dismantling
their structures one botanical item
at a time, discarding the petals
that were serving as ballet dress,
until they stood slim and lank,
as stringy as mandrakes, stripped
right down to their green peduncles.
It was a sorry lesson in female form.
In those days we were not taught
how orgasms are made – pulling
flowers apart was as far as sex
education went in the colonies.

MISTS AND FRUITFULNESS

Autumn is such a total commitment,
surrounding us, like every season,
right to the very tips of each day;
leaf-wreckage, bonfire and blue sky
become our absolute life condition,
and yet it's so parochial – from space
our autumn is just a brown tide-line
swaying up and down the planet,
a band of discoloration hardly visible
fifty miles distant from the earth;
autumns are scattered throughout
the galaxy, local smears on the flanks
of sun-circling bodies; one engine-burn
would lift us clear beyond all seasons.

DROMEDARIS, REIJGER, GOEDE HOOP

I'm no authority on colonial shipping
so cannot say what their holds held
that drove the native people kneewards,
and bound them to perpetual contract.
Their keels scraped on coral ecologies;
their crews had few words for what they saw,
none for kindness. Eventually vegetations
and escarpments found linguistic footing
in their mingled lexicons, but it was too late –
there's no return to pre-linguistic purity.
Will a fustian language do, one smelling
of book mould, rusted press-machinery?
So watch us while we melt the old type,
redream history in bright rhetorical lead.

RIGHT VENTRICULAR CARDIOMYOPATHY

That cardiac disturbance announces itself
like a flutter of rain against the windowpanes,

a light wince of muscular contractions
as soft as the swallowing action of a throat;

a ripple of small, felted hammers drumming
on the wires of a cardio-vascular concert piano;

a plucking of heart-strings, a feathery stroke
on the pericardium of a skittish harpsichord;

a minor puff upsets the science of the heart,
teases out the wrong reaction, gives a nudge,

a triggering jolt to the delicate electronics
strung tremblingly over stretches of muscle;

a quiver going against the ventricular grain,
contrary to custom – one strike and you're out.

AMPLIFICATION

The microphone shines its beam
into every corner of my voice;
its bright electronic insistencies
isolate tongue, tooth and larynx,
infuse visibility into every click,
glide, pop and fizz of language;
the acoustic magnifier probes into
the back of my mouth, extracting
every particle of sound, polishing it
with deeper resonance; a buzzing
inflates the vowels to concavity,
rounding them off; drum-taps hit
the enamel shells of consonants,
and the molars of my voice grind.

VOYAGES OF DISCOVERY

That Portuguese body to be worked:
the language slithering out of her mouth
like a birth, an offering up of Lisbon,
the cakes and the fado and the trams,
the coffee houses where Fernando sat.
The whispering and lisping consonants
of her Lusian dialect to be worked
as passage on a steamer across divides,
over equators and cultures, athwart
sexual differences, the asymmetries
inviting convergence and interlocking.
Then moving in glandular bonding:
the sea-swell, the perfumed coastlines,
the bush – smells of arousal and arrival.

TUTTI

A wild fly the size of my room blew in.
I was right inside the fly's auditorium –
occupying the best seat in the house.
The fly was a baritone – I could feel
its tuba metals and its oboe ebonies
tickling me. Inclusion in the fly's dizzy
physiognomy meant being buzzed silly
by the waters wrinkling its ear-canals;
my phonetic holes and acoustic bones
trilled with sympathetic string frictions;
at the centre of its orchestra was the fly
itself, a soft black pearl of frenzied Paganini;
I widened the crack under the window a
smidgen and its entire philharmonia flowed out.

FISHES IN BOOKS

How many objects that have never existed
are formed and fired in the kilns of reasoning?
I return to sea-books as my locus of the real –
spirit-breathing fish bodies inverting actuality;
as colourful as carp these imaginary species
swim behind our eyes in pure concept-space;
ichthyologists of nothingness, we study these
vivid eccentrics, documenting behaviour as raw
as the practical brutes of the commercial sea-
world in that Irvin and Johnson sticker-book
I was given one Christmas – full of industrial
tunnies, big sea-thugs hauled onto ugly trawlers,
destined for canning factories and supermarkets;
my fabricated kabeljou are just as cold and fishy.

JAPANESE DAGGER

I ponder the sweep and edge of a steel
ceremonial dagger from Japan, its blade
engraved with clouds, lyre birds and carp,
its lacquered scabbard tipped with pewter.
What services has this weapon performed
in the course of its instrumental lifetime?
Has it ever put a human being to death?
That would seem to be its main purpose –
it will have been engineered to do harm,
to slice or stab inch-deep red gashes into
human flesh; anything short of murder,
sacrifice or suicide would be a betrayal
of its intended destiny, the terrible beauty
of its execution, its premeditated evil.

ENGLISH IN AFRICA

We took the language of the Europeans
and cauterised it, laughing at its prolixity –
where they would rub two sticks together
to make living fire, we just struck a match.
We beat their high vowels flat on the anvils
of new phonetic forges and muses of dirt.
To cure their pale linguistics into soundings
more in keeping with our burnt savannahs
we joined the salts of the Southern Ocean
to smoky notes of Karoo herbs. We spiked
our vocabularies with the gargled alphabet
of the Cape Namaquas, our fellow Africans –
who took one look at our pale complexions
and called us Europeans – we gasped at the insult.

URBAN IGLOO

In your ice-box apartment in Dundee
a severely plucked library was cornered
into a few volumes of Plath and Hughes
to stave off the silence; aside from that
an elaborate chiming necklace that could
not refrain from highly-strung jingling
as soon as handled; you had to lower it
back into its basket to stop the acoustic
chattering – there its plates and shells
coiled down into a dull metallic puddle
of pewterish links and chains. Books read
in that temperature, dug from sarcophagal
cold, spoke to us of remote gulags; their
stilled yells were tiny protests glued in ice.

IN/OUT

Some well-travelled air is sucked aside
into a damp anatomical cul-de-sac
of fibrous wind-bags – this air has been
everywhere, drawn through the perfumed
yellow brushes of autumn, scented by
the lungs of crows and squirrels, forced
into service by leaf-blowers, scooping
gases and chemicals from the fermenting
crusts of organic residues; thus charged
with its rough nose of molecules it visits
us, swims through our breathing channels
and inflates us to a moment of the finest
counterpoise, a muscular tipping point;
then spent puffs are wheezed back into play.

TANGLED IN THE METAPHYSICS OF TIME

Two machines assembled into the same
body or casing are like a Swiss clock and
petrol engine, for example, both sharing
certain cylinders, the one's chiming
driving the other's pistons, the other's
locomotion winding the other's springs;
or one of those clocks whose seconds
are plucked out of the escapement like
quills fingering harpsichord strings;
the red and blue circulatory threads
of entangled twins, a single blood system
shared like a moebius strip – so time
and me are implicated in each other like
two laundries tumbling in the same drum.

NATIVE TO THE ISLANDS

I stand clear of the influence of islands.
Gigantic hinterland trees surround me,
trees that need lots of interior to screw
their heavy plumbing into stable earth.
Scottish island cultures keep their distance:
the guitar music of old fishermen, creels,
lobsterpots and willow-woven crab pots,
crofts anchored like molars in coastal rocks.
I cannot truly lay claim to any of these,
know nothing of them in my native blood;
they do not swim along its kinship-veins.
There are no Gaelic places in my brain.
No bloodlines trace me back to old women
humming woollen hats on wooden looms.

THE PLEASURES OF READING AND CLASSICAL LEARNING IN CHINA
"Books are as sexy as women" – Yang Xiong (53 BC-AD 18)

Everything that is sensual in the world –
from the taste of Mexican blood oranges
to the narcoleptic numbness of sleep –
is concentrated in the human body.
Its pickup systems are more acute than
bugging devices planted in a dissident's
Moscow apartment. Soft-hued galaxies fall
onto the rounds of the eye, its ragged-
rimmed iris, its black-eye pupil, and open
inside the brain like a flu tablet's cloudy
smokings. Oils from a reader's hands linger
on books, a woman's saliva on the lips of
her lover. The body's welcoming secretions
correctly guess the depravity of our nerves.

PLEIADE

The culture and anatomy of the mopani tree
prepared you for French literature even before
you knew the language. It was in you
waiting like a tough, coiled seed ready
to unfold its historic, ancestral DNA.
Blesséd were you to be standing in Setswana
realms full of hints going far beyond
mere botany and climatology. Particulars
were already anticipated by pages left blank
in the notebooks of Swedish naturalists.
Ronsard and Du Bellay were there in embryo,
a predisposition which made it impossible
to take trees in their pure native boscage.
Nature sang a different tune, always human.

FLIP-FLOP

Strong and weak beats –
my club-footed heart
limps through my body,
sending the shake of its
faltering into neck and wrist.
I measure myself
by counting the pulse
of real seconds in box-
time, dry Euclidean
periods that reprimand
the wet biological time
my body slithers in.
Like a fried-egg watch
my heart is a dada flop.

THE REAL WORK

A vexing anonymity surrounds
the stateless-by-conviction maker –
nation-building is set to one side
like an iron threshing machine
rusting beside the immaculate wheat.

International activism may succeed
before it too comes to earth like Mir,
scratching five straight lines of burn
through the upper atmosphere.

That leaves the snowflakes falling
with puffs of white like pop-corn
popped from waterdrops – work becomes
the struggle of a conscientious mind
to invent new metaphors for snow.

LANDING A SHIT-HOUSE ON THE MOON
(it's not as hard as you might think)

With only a % of earth's gravity to fight
against, all it took was a few gentle puffs
of jet propulsion to lower the bristly lunar
vehicle onto the surface of the moon.
No atmosphere equals no foul weather
and no turbulence; hence that dreamlike
parabolic glide of a machine requiring
no aerodynamic modelling to steady it;
you could land a rickety old farmyard
shit-house on the moon if you wanted to;
piloting it down would have given those
gnarly cosmonauts no trouble at all, despite
its ventilation holes shaped like a moon,
its splintery door banging open and shut.

A QUESTION FOR THE DAWN

The irreconcilable charm of daybreak
is a question fading like a slow glissando
of light that lingers on even in the most
conclusive arrival of dawn – in dazzling
daytime a diaphanous wafer of moon;
every moment gives a new threshold
to cross, further deferrals; so many
rightful claimants are using the hours
(their hours) to pour wing-power across
the sky, make contractual hops through
the lattices of a winter-flowering cherry;
a wake of trembling branches shows
the passage of the magpie, its progress
marked by raucous cries of ownership.

CARDIOMYOPATHY

Looking into the body is like
looking directly into the sun:
its intense, unshielded workings
are too serious for the devices
which perform the looking,
overwhelmed in their corneal
and iris structures – as tender
as the delicate manifolds in
a fish's gills; laws rigid enough
to pin down chemistry labs
also govern our bodies, and
one day will lower them limp
with organ failure – cardiology's
not for the faint-hearted.

GIGOLO

Iron weights keep the gentleman's physique
taut as the sails of a clipper pulled upright
by inflating airstreams, and ready him for
his offer of the Full Boyfriend Experience.
Involving more than (but also not less than)
fifteen minutes of good anatomical sex
this might include wine and roses, pre-dinner
banter and compliments on her outer beauty.
But I notice that his preparations don't go
as far as grooming his brains with Socrates
or dry-reading witty scenes of faux gallantry
in Moliere to tone his conversational muscles –
those culminating fifteen physical minutes
are clearly what's in the forefront of his mind.

EXERCISE REGIME

Once, our faces were clamped to the skull
like limpets onto rock; that healthy suck
of pressure kept the features in shape;
now they hang slack as old lounge curtains;
our hilarious bodies provoke the disbelief
of the young, who think that every muscle
can be remade by exercise, exercise, exercise;
they think we have willed our decrepitude,
that it's only sheer lack of enterprise or wit
that stops us from gymming, slimming and jogging
our hopeless figures back to sensual youth,
back to the peak of astronauts in their capsule
viewing the earth as it's never been seen before
with eyes as round and blue as the planet.

IN A HIDE

Only when my body has powered off
its auxiliary systems, and stopped
chewing, shuffling, sniffing & scratching –
shutting itself down level after level
until all it does is breathe and attend –
only then does language drift back to me
in single words, followed by wedded pairs,
then whole grammatical flights of them
like the return of scared-off birds,
the trickle-back of shy ground-animals,
until confident populations of sound
settle full-voiced over the area
and flowerless trees fill with the squeals
of a hundred, tiny, rusted wheels.

I HAVE READ *WATT*

What have I read *Watt*?
I have read *Watt* scuffed
and sunned, speckled
and loose in its binding.
I have read *Watt* from
mint to falling apart.
I have read *Watt* cocked
and bowed, to slightly
foxed and bumped.
I have read *Watt* to
the usual library markings
and ballpoint underlining.
I have read *Watt* warped,
rubbed and in stitches.

THE COMMON PEOPLE

Even the humblest folk have to be
as tough as African foot-soles,
be able to turn like the backlash
of a cobra; squally weather has
been sequestered under their skins;
various errors of mother-judgement
and upbringing have made them
inoculated, impervious, immune,
proud sporters of stony expressions;
but sometimes they have to make
complete arseholes of themselves: cry,
give speeches, do the foxtrot; it's that
constant tripping between extremes
that makes them so fascinating to us.

A WOMAN OF YEARS

Her face bears traces of the thoughts
of many years, a grainy deposit
held back on filtering muslins;
her features have sifted so many ideas
a glow of opinion has remained
on her skin, giving her appearance
an air of pondering; her expression
even in repose is busy considering
what just happened; this constant
communing of her mind with itself
means her face never switches off;
it's always mulling over some far
from welcome evidence, is always
just about to put itself into words.

RETURN FROM THE ISLANDS

Somewhere a difference has been made.
Your sentences carry the sound of island
names in them like a blue dye in language.
Chafed by extremes your skin has the fiery
coldness of bracken, bundles of sodden moss,
night as black as the stars. There is wilderness
in your look where your glance has caught
the gestural cries of hunting birds, foamy
threads of runoff slipping down through
the scaly stems of reptilian heather rooted
like claws in the bearded earth. Your hands
recall the pull of spiky plants. Horizons
tilt within your eyes, your nerves hold onto
the plunge and drive of small Scottish seas.

HOMUNCULUS

I was old enough read Kant's *Critique*
but emotionally no older than a foetus –
a tight-as-a-bud creature curled like
a prawn, eyes still covered with skin,
my sexual organs an ambiguous bump,
drinking amniotic fluid from my fingers.
If many sunrises had not opened me
what chance had a woman's wooing,
her premature coaxing, on that green
blastula as hard as a brussels sprout?
She couldn't unpeel its clinging layers
for all her concupiscence and fingernails.
One day a cellular dawning deep within;
until then, the closed fist of the foetus.

THE ILLUSION ROOM

To read a poem is to dwell for a time
in a tilted room where the psychology
is all wrong; the floors are angled skew,
the ceiling makes you duck and crouch;
the room exerts, it makes you brace
yourself against a slant which isn't there;
it tips you up like crockery off a tea-tray;
it makes you disappear under floorboards
into a pipework of rambling sentences;
its gravity sucks away at your ears, pulls
your personality in opposing directions;
you groan and gurgle in the plumbing
of its bad grammar, your eyes dispute
the geometry they can't agree upon.

NAVIGATION IN GREEN WATER

I guide my little boat of understanding
into your waters, in dark, Puritan January.
In these post-Christian days, your oceans
are ruled by an unfavourable cosmos,
one contrary to my interests – enigmatic
stars in your heavens, uncongenial gods
holding office, promulgating cold orders;
upturned Christmas trees on the pavements,
with browning extremities, shorn of
their trivial joys and outgrown meanings,
put out of doors, lying on their sides
like methylated tramps – unaccommodated
in Bethlehem. The jib tautens, the braced hull
slips tight, controlled, through whipped seas.

A STOIC'S INJUNCTION

Unpleasant encounters are the weft
and woof of daily existence – exult
in the contrariness of people, your own body,
the stubborn withholdings of the world;
a knot of sea-drift is keeping its secrets
even though you have given it a home
on your desk – you are not significant
enough to be the recipient of its tales;
welcome that awkward pain – this is
the texture of life, something to brace
yourself against, and push, and feel
the sinewy mechanisms of your body lock
and tighten, with consciousness, resolve,
in your struggle with the angel of chance.

AT THE MERCY

Something at least is rational, a one-man
skiff subject to the usual nautical codes;
but the rest is hot worlds being born
beneath that single sail and tiller,
melting and freezing to planetary
rhythms, the vast physics of soft cores,
gravities, ellipses, proximation to stars;
volcanoes spurt from the caked mantle,
frost bristles, continental edges crackle;
you have to face the world, the social *monde*,
with all these indigestions bubbling inside,
and nothing allowed to be shown of them,
except on the eyes, over whose surface
the mariner's white clouds race like panic.

COLD AND CROWS

Crows in the bitter air transact
their imploring cries; stubborn
blue applies relentless consistency
to immoveable sky; the feathered
animals impose normality on cold,
make their bodies bearable with down,
fledge, fluff, plumage and pinion;
their swart serrated cries release
vital warmth from their hearts
and bellies; desperate calls break
ice, crack the freezing; the day skims
off these resources, punishing over-
investment; not all voices make it,
or squeak through to another day.

COMPARATIVE RELIGION

A deal struck with our dangerous god
by experienced deity negotiators
means we never have to tell the truth
unless we've stepped inside a dark
wooden box containing a priest.
Devoutness impels us to erect
vast propitiatory architectures
with enough candles of beeswax
and tallow to keep any faith alive
for a thousand years or more –
and yet how easily we lost ground
to a new brand of zealots, ones
who eat only with the right hand
and pray with their bums in the air.

LIFE BROUGHT INTO THE HOUSE

Once you brought an elm tree into the house;
another time it was a hamster for my birthday;
most recently it was the grey, fledgling crow.
We planted the elm in woods as dark as witchcraft –
now it's lost among trees like an unmarked grave;
the hamster scythed obsessive crescents of paper
from my poetry books to line its prison cage;
the crow at last forgot what crows looked like;
its eyes turned blue, then white, and then it died.

Don't bring any more living things into my house.
Anything you bring inside must be long dead
and gone. Death is after all the default condition
of things; let us therefore not elevate the living
above dead crows or mortal elms, above stones.

FULL IMMERSIVE RESPONSE

The weather hardens and tightens;
illusions of philanthropy evaporate;
benevolence becomes implausible
as the sky narrows and intensifies;
coldness and wetness, with wind
to drive it against the pale body,
is gathering in a steady topple
of inevitability; a clenching of
vapours and humours, a fit of
bunched and knotted muscularity
is in progress on scales more total
than our human way; to survive it
we'll have to submit, and breathe
the arriving storm into our lungs.

WEAPONS OF THE FRIENDLY ISLANDS

I must express these rough berries
into colourless, empty nouns, the way
primitive hunters rub local stuff
into their gear to season it, make
it durable, flexible, or – as may be – rigid.
Slowly they collect their lures, barbs,
like something a dream leaves
under your pillow – it has marinaded
for ages in waxings, finger impressings,
squintings up and down the long curve.
Now it is ready for its terrible work.
It has been so beautifully crafted
that the blood of its victims is always
on the hunter, never on the weapon.

VANISHING APES

A blue line went through the Barbary apes;
they rang some naval bell or other,
were someone's literary cargo in wooden crates;
I couldn't trust them not to be
spoiled perishables, shelf-rubbed, second-hand;
they with their hard, restless
monkey-bodies, all muscularity and movement,
they deserved better than to be
the innocent victims of irresponsible allusion;
and perhaps illegally trapped,
unquarantined, carriers of dazzling green viruses,
they might have posed a health risk.
Until I recall that these purely subjunctive apes,
once written out, would have vanished
not only from the record, but from reality itself.

A COMMON ROAD

If our two bloods could be sluiced
into one circulation, to balance out
our inequalities and find their level
like different waters brought together
in chemical apparatus, the columns
coming to rest in adjacent beakers
at the same number etched onto
the glass of graduated cylinders,
that would be nice, a local solution
that could be rolled out to blood-
pairing clinics throughout the land.
That would be an equality grounded
in medical science, and sealed with
cannulas, needles, plastic feed-lines.

A GLANS SONNET

The old acorn-maker strains
and blows the hard knobbles
out of itself into thousands of
scattered locations where sprigs
are freshest and greenest:
there, lumps and bunions form
which would betoken gum disease
or elm mortality in different
climes but here herald the joy
of little hermaphrodites squeezed
from under the skin of the plant
(as salamanders pop out of mud);
the pips grow helmets and hoods
all plump and glistening and tight.

ALBERTINE ASLEEP

Should I be ashamed at finding
her hearing-disability attractive,
at wanting to kiss her dumbness,
those lips from which no word
can come out entirely correct;
to feel in my mouth the special
muscular struggles of her tongue,
the over-vowelling of her words,
the consonants loudly plucked from
her palate and the back of her teeth?
I would want to feel her speaking
onto my lips, to feel the imperfect
flutter of her dumb phonetics
pass her hearing loss into my mouth.

METATARSUS VARIES

Today you let me touch your swollen foot,
puffy and tender at the base of the toes –
that old condition of yours flaring up.
It was hard to squeeze the shoe back on
so you let me help by doing up the strap,
leaning across you casually and intimately,
sharing thereby a wry acknowledgement
of our midlife's stiffness and stoutness,
though sternly forbidden to stroke your ankle!
There was as much in those secret permissions
hidden from the eyes of nearby colleagues
as complete nakedness, full acts of sex:
your slipped-off shoe, my pitying touches,
discreetly in the crowded coffee lounge.

DIALECT OF THE TRIBE

A certain homeliness escapes
adequate expression, despite vacant
skies, perennial berg profiles;
something corresponds, something
almost verbal, on the tongue-tip
of language, to that very thing
out there for which there are
no words adequate, a matching
something which is struggling
with impotent linguistic forces
to form the words for speaking it,
to fashion its phonetic counterpart,
to bed itself in the conceptual
earthwork of living vocabulary.

IN A FRENCH FIELD

I'm not really standing in this coppice
with its tree-leaves silvered like centimes
by the level sun, its dry rustle of mice;
I'm at my desk in Edinburgh scratching
English sentences onto a papery void;
the cold and coining light is a compound
of late season coupled with declining day;
straight plough-grooves sweep down
from me through claggy velvet farm-soil;
not only have I never been here before
the place is just an onion-string of nouns;
now bird noises are heading off for night,
and I'm not sure how I'll be getting home
but I'm guessing that you don't give a damn.

WEDDING CEMETERY

Like two reluctant armies, the new graves
advance from either end of the field.

"The Cemetery Expansion", Maurice Riordan

When the two graveyards meet
after expanding towards each other
from opposite ends of the parish
what jubilation, what a clasping
of knuckly hands underground;
what courtships then, conducted
blindly under the soil like moles,
by touch, never surfacing into air;
eventually what progeny born from
hundred-year couplings of bones,
baby corpses fattening like potatoes;
and finally what dying again, darker
than the old, more absolute, to depths
from which there is no coming back.

STONE WORLD

Holding a planet in
the palm of my hand
as cold and solid as
a pebble with mineral
markings, its russet
ferrous weathers
streaked like Jupiter
with storm bands;
hard to credit
massive worlds
self-contained
in freckled space.
This almost wins
my faith in stars.

THE CONCEPT OF NATURE

Smeared with daubs of clarity
the cloud-normed morning
inches towards totality;
time is the unfinished work,
sucking the world in after it,
living in the comet-tail
of moiling vortices scaled down
to endurable slowness;
within this dawdle, a chance
for poetry and kindness;
in construction fields
far beyond humanity
the crane-fly sets down
frail legs and wings
onto the digger's blade.

THE EARTH OUR DWELLING PLACE

Our home is the cracked earth
riven and wrinkled into canyons
and kloofs like a shrunken apple
and then plugged with plants;
on elated cliff-rock elevations
dotted with euphorbias one sheds
clothes and Copernicus, table
manners and the times tables;
birds and koggelmanders trickle
and slither over halfmens trees
and aloes hang on by their feet;
ears fill with insect shrilling,
eyes grow full as granaries; such
dwelling lasts but hours at best.

UIT DIE HANTAM

Remnants of a previous country persist
as neurological fragments and fictions,
false wiring in the brain, gunge-coated
contact-points in the neural junction box;
wind brushing itself over heather grass
garners emotional musks and pungencies,
a half-articulate incense of childhood;
lavender and rose aren't rich enough
to bring forth images or language;
failing full embodiment, the epiphany
remains in bud, in cocoon, in blastula;
smells, flowers, mountain backs likened
to extinct blue dinosaurs keep their clear
declarations locked in deepest chemistry.

BIRD FEEDERS TO THE RESCUE

Fat-balls and nutritive bundles
of meal mushed with insects
sustain the undiscriminating birds,
birds with promiscuous hygiene,
low food standards, and urges
to outlive the next British winter;
we're talking about, as well
they know, sparrows, nut-hatches,
robins and sparrow-hawks
diverted from their aerial kill;
corncrakes, wrens and loons
can go to hell; as can ostriches,
who'd gulp down a whole day's
seed supply in a single swallow.

EXPUNGED

Mist like a tsunami of oblivion rears
behind the buildings – it is advancing
or retreating – too slowly to tell which;
it is the oblivion of matter itself, when
reality goes blank and forgets its being –
it disappears into its full counterfactual
absence, into the never-was; connections
to what's left over are severed straight off
like the side of a building ripped open
by this morning's news; consequences
jut causelessly into the visible present,
riddled with duct mechanisms sucking
their fluids from nothing; if advancing,
its nothing includes me and this poem.

SUSPICIONS OF THE ANCESTRAL APE

Kept regular on hard, fibrous vegetables
the ape maintains its primal magnificence,
a squat wrestler nurtured on nuts, berries,
soft fruit and the red pulp of monkeys.
Like a fist clenching and unclenching itself
it moves daily through the arduous canopy.
It cannot smell our philosophy, or realise
the awesome implications of Being and Reality.
But far along the evolutionary line it hears
faint echoes of the arriving human mind,
the hammering of industry and politics.
It can almost smell the soldering of circuits
and the diesel fumes of logging trucks gunned
through devastated rainforest by the new ape.

RAW PHILOSOPHY OF MIRACLES

Miracles so exceed the laws
of visualisation, of sensing,
of ordinary encounter, they
could be happening right now
under our very eyes, their scribble
of law-violation so extreme
they escape our notice: language
doesn't have grammar enough
to describe them, reason itself
is blind both to their upshot
and to their very occurrence;
they are shaking the foundations
of our existence without leaving
the slightest trace of themselves.

A DESCENT OF MAN

Dropping down through living layers
we traverse successive University
Faculties, as our materials become
rarefied and more scientific, and fogs
of biology thin out as we descend
below sea worms, fish-mammals
and luminous galactic blastulas;
inside us a natural cybernetics starts:
silicon, electricity, filament, lattice,
and finally the metals and minerals
of elemental atoms arrive, their pure
fire hinting at final abstraction when
all the machinery and nomenclature
of the gritty world is left far behind.

THE GRASS CAMPAIGNS

A cereal ambiguity shows in the deportment
of spears and tongues of grass, tensile design
in green materials bundled into long vessels;
simple manufacturing processes under the skin
are converting carbon dioxide to sugar –
like the hard-wearing industries magnifying
chemical reactions to a commercial level
in box-ugly, wind-angled Port Elizabeth;
I used to smell that burning sweetness over
North End, when school hadn't yet grown
me up into army recruit and raw student;
I snapped their stalks for solace, allies since
the grain bins of Egypt and seven thin kine
in the cautionary dreams of the overlord.

MORTARLESS CITIES OF CENTRAL AFRICA

Dusk has pasted ligament and webbing
between the buildings, a calciferous growth
blunting and dulling their exact structural
definitions usually so gracile and fastidious
in sunlight. A civilization stands or falls by
the weather that turns up on visiting days.
Large agricultural stockades in semi-dressed
stone seem an archaeological oversight from
ancient African cities – red anthills and silver
thorn trees steal the limelight in Zimbabwe;
glittering hills perpetuate devastations from
the stone-dry city – lame ruin is everywhere;
termites have chomped through the lyric poetry
on surmised bark or papyrus, coating it all red.

SOLAR ALCHEMIES

Alchemies of young morning push the boundaries
of good sense; early sunlight thinks outside
the box, with plenty of hydrogen to spare,
inventing a supplementary world as fragile
as frost, due for evaporation when warmer
certainties arrive – fiscal and remunerating
institutions assembling their flannel anti-bodies;
now it's the turn of the horizontal, treetop-
skimming sun to push the envelope; briefly
photons pop their excitements against peels
of effervescence; claddings of parkland
and domicile assert their civilized interiors,
as busy as churches sporting pyxes, thuribles
and small suicide-worshipping congregations.

PAMELA IN HER BODY

Pamela is talking out of her masses;
I know she's in there somewhere,
inside that body not doing what
she'd prefer it to do; physiognomy
that was wholly subject to reason
would not be so productive of itself
or be so aggressively about to get
out of hand and start imposing its
masterful weight. Pamela's eyes are
doing their level best to make it all
seem normal, but it's not; the worst
has happened – the years have turned
up, as we knew they would, and this
is the body they've brought with them.

ORDNANCE LOST OVERBOARD

A 40-pounder skids off the deck; first
(back up a bit) tilts its wheels at the rails
then topples plop-heavy into the marble
freckling of the swells; it goes down
in the imaginations of all those watching,
sinks through the aquatic strata of their
minds, into the depths each has furnished
according to his own audacity and education
over the years; for some that will be a mini-
aquarium with a tiny submerged Scottish
castle and some evergreen plastic weeds;
for others it will be more or less authentic
oceanography, full of pressure dials; for all
it beds down in mythology's deepest mud.

CLARINET DROPSY IN DALMENY KIRK

The humid musician is struggling to keep
her clarinet dry, as lung-dampened foehns
infiltrate its joints and moisten the pads,
coating the inner ebony core with a silver
sweat of condensation; the body's waste
monoxide gases serve so many functions
on the way out – a by-product of breathing
from the bronchial sponges diverted into
music, vibrating our own language reeds
in passing, and carrying our minds outdoors
into speech; the warm mouth blows words
and melodies into the chilly atmospheres
of a country church, expelling spent beads
of steam through a black exhaust-cylinder.

THE FIERCE WHEAT IN SAMUEL PALMER

Every day falls open at the right place,
spread full and flat like a heavy journal.
Rook pairs stand perfectly modelled in fields
tilted at roof angles. Yellow broom signals
the abiding of Albion and of rare Jerusalem
in successions of plant life and summer air.
Each day offers room for achieving things in,
but what? Obviously, like Garibaldi,
you can land on the divided Italian coast,
your snaking, pike-haired columns making
a strong impression on even a very large day.
But those are career moves, don't explain
why beautiful, eye-leaved Egyptian bushes
waylay us with unnecessary abundance.

LUNAR THEATRE

The moon, beginning as dark urine orange,
rises with progressively purified yellows,
until, nearly white gold or dazzling chalk,
suspends itself with a sense of religious
theatre directly above the church's steeple;
it is an apotheosis – something absolute;
and then a blink, a slippage, a spill from
the apex as it shifts sideways off its perch –
the great occasion has already started to decay;
ordinary angles, commonplace orientations
take over from destiny's perfect alignments;
like a bent metal arm the displaced moon
is widening its arc, putting pure scientific
distance between itself and the snubbed spire.

MEASURES

The day ticks by, using changes of light
sweeping through degrees of dilution
and density; transition's motions
are indiscernible, even the biological
periods in an aphid's body are not fine
enough; an oak tree's bloodstream
creeps more slowly than the shadows
sliding up its trunk; a week passes
before its thirst is entirely assuaged;
the heavens are metronomes shedding
planetary hours in breathings of light;
after brief inattention a long porous
femur of cloud has formed in the sky
like the floating bones of hippopotami.

LIBRARY SESSION 531

I need her sniffle to force my concentration,
as poets need stress-metrics to force invention.
Our mantra is you can't afford to be precious –
write through the wrong pen, on a wobbly desk,
with distractions of mist veiling and unveiling
some magical hills (let me not distract myself),
write though your heart is breaking, etc.
Here is the time, now is the place – your body
and your brain's inadvertencies are all
you have to go on; this is what the suitcase has
been packed for – now go and make the journey.
Far below, something has begun to chew concrete.
I can almost smell the petrol on its breath.
Oceanic green sets the hills ablaze with words.

SHOES IN THE CHARITY SHOP

These have already broken in one pair
of feet; the previous wearer still stands
in them like an invisible column of air;
now, like a sold horse, the shoes must get
used to a different weight and rhythm.
Old people's bodies stick out from
the past, are the protruding tip of long
existence; they are sunk like shafts into
a forgotten moisture; their roots drill
through a ceiling of pebbly rubble into
a subterranean world of defunct sunshine
where monochrome trams clank along
streets slowed down by cobbles, and people
with old radio accents politely beg to differ.

THOUSAND YEAR REIGNS

The trees' barbarian hoards of copper
and gold are scarcely worth a glance today:
the plate, the bangles and the crowns,
the medallions and bling of Saxon kings,
in coarse, explicit, clumsy metalwork,
are gone; rags of old investitures remain.

Now thick-hided enchanted animals are rooted
to the spot; their long Reichs are over;
their Ciceronian eloquence, their splendid
prose, their golden rhetoric – all bluster now;
their wizard-loaned speech has been withdrawn;
they're back to the grunts they were born with.

Humbler than dogs, densely unintelligent,
they lift their magnificent unresistence to the skies.

FIRST THING

Was it to de-sex me first thing each day
that she incited my horn and sucked out
the marrow – ensuring my eyes were lustreless
until evening towards anyone but herself?
Or did she just love filling my body with
orgasms, like stuffing a storage jar full
of brightly coloured marbles? It awed me
that the juice of her fellatio still circulated
in her body hours after I had dumped her
for the first time. I behaved capriciously;
she was steadfast in refusing golden showers.
No blame either way, I'm sure – I like to
think that give and take balance themselves
out in these cases. But I could be wrong.

FIELD NATURALIST IN SITU

Clouds retract like a reptile's eye-shutter
leaving stingingly blue skies for the sun
to dazzle in – an intense optic nerve where
all light goes to get processed into objects.
For example, if I talk about crackerjack toads
you'd imagine I was sitting in a swamp;
actually I'm to be found in my usual Library
of Congress shelf location. Yes, it's all very
lexical in here; we're all long-term victims
of childhood reading abuse, most of whose
bibliophiles are dead or electronically tagged.
Still, swamp-juice is creeping into my socks
and the toads are pinging like plastic spatulas
which is something that toads do really well.

ROUGH GULLY BASH

The embankment's abrasive meshwork
of barbed-wire brambles frightens off
with thorn & thistle, spike & bristle –
whoever presses on will be taking home
poisonous burrowing hairs, burning rash.
The river below, probably also poisoned,
by scarlet algae and starved crocodiles,
has come to a sluggish halt like the bubble
in a spirit level, at the apex of the tipping-
table of the escarpment. Observant minds
break apart like light fanned on pyramids
of glass – some page through botany manuals
to match leaf with leaf, ably assisted by
a little Greek. Others consult their eyes.

LIVING ON THE MOON

You're still yes-yessing me, shining that
probationary light into our myopic future.
What to do next? Self-confessed children
as we are in all this, we've taken out insurance
against our ineptitude, certain weaknesses
we carry with us, where life has severed us
from ourselves with invisible cuts, stare
how we may into the mirror of psychiatry.
Shifts in our culture have given us existence
beyond marriage – we're living where others
have not been before, opened-up extensions
of our bodies. Onto the grey, unplanted
soil we set footsteps, one at a time, with not
an apple, snake or agenda-rigging god in sight.

A POSY OF SMELLS

You sat surrounded by sweetpea and honeysuckle
brought back from the countryside by your daughter.
Odours, essences of flowers and vegetables, fumed
out of their hard, friendly bodies and delighted you.
My day had not been one of sweetpea and honeysuckle.
Firstly my lovely poetry manuscript was turned down
by Flarestack Poets – an occupational hazard, I guess.
Next I learnt our recent leaks were caused by metal
thieves having prised the lead sheeting from our roof.
Finally I spelt the word 'wrack' instead of 'rack' when
texting to say I was 'wracking my brains' over Cicero –
'wrack', you said, was seaweed on the beach. But then
you promised us a seaweed bath in Ireland, hot and oily –
and suddenly my day, too, was crowned by fragrances.

MERE HEAVENLY WALKING

Movements achieved through the body,
its joints and hinges and oily musculature,
are smoothed and consecrated by last
night's passion – love beautifies the materials
of its nature, does something lax and lovely
to its utilitarian loops and busy bags
or pear-dense blobs of technology.
Everything swivels and sags and strokes
moist component against component, relishing
its mere existence in covering mere ground.
Finely-tuned skin competes with purring
engine-organs for extremes of beatitude.
Panther-padding feet place fulsome
and consummated weight upon the earth.

INITIATION RAPTURE

That hymen rupture unites us,
I now realise years afterwards.
To have taken part together
in that immemorial, species-old
ritual, dictated by the workings
of our primate biology, was
both privilege and necessity.
Unwitnessed by any members
of our community, that tribe
which takes such an interest
in these crossings, we shared
the sacred breaking of your body.
I will never cease to wear
your ripped and bloody ring.

WHO WAS THE PROPHET'S MOTHER?

Mary Mother of God what was her name again?
It was a way of sorting the U from the non-U,
the angora goats from the karakul sheep.
Too little knowledge had become a dangerous thing.
The hostages were converting in huddled groups
in the fresh produce aisle, beside the Rice Crispies.
Some were still frantically cramming new creed
just seconds before the big question laid its
chillingly warm muzzle against their foreheads.
It was a while before the first policeman was shot.
A bullet tore the beliefs clean out of his head.
A full scoop of dogmas came out on that occasion
like the wet clot of pips in a paw-paw.
That changed his mind pretty swiftly.

POET TO SOCIAL WORKER

Psychology's as physical as lungs
and shinbones. Language is the same –
fashioned out of cartilage and teeth.
Those are the materials we work in.
You might as well be a country vet,
your arms slathered to the elbows
in fresh cow slobber – it's that visceral,
working with people, with semi-organic
entities like families and foster parents.
Social work, like surgery and midwifery,
takes you into the entrails of the human.
Rolling viscous black ink onto the disc
of my Adana to make words visible,
I feel pristine, clean, slightly precious.

IN THE THREAD OF COMPTE

A hard rind of light contains
the world this morning, making
surfaces be all that there is
of what there is, a callous
fibrous covering that carries
all of the meat of the inner object.
A porcelain gloss, a leathery
fullness are all the resisted eye
encounters, leaving the mind
in doubt of anything behind.
Appearance has thickened,
swelled itself out to subsume
the reality of the thing, a world
all fat light and outwardness.

LIKE A SOUTH-FACING WINDOW

Of yellow glass the leaves –
so susceptible to light
they are – admitting and
tinting the rays flicking
through the jocund panes
joggling like the coloured
diamond shapes of motley.
Like an octopus taking
on the deceptive camouflage
of a clown the tree shakes
squares of glass dyed
with many mirthful hues.
Light slips through that
fleet and fly transparency.

STILL MORNING WITH BIRDFLIGHT

The day's dead still – the slowest nautical speed
a boat can travel, but these aren't boats –
they're trees, have never travelled, and never
more slowly than now – their stillness realised
in thousands of separate instances, one per leaf;
not just one immobile sail, hanging down
from the mast in limp and breathless air,
but fleets and fleets of drooping linen.
No, that wasn't a tremor or a twitch in them
like the uncontrollable spasm of a soldier
standing to attention on a stiff parade;
it was a bird, dashing across the face
of all this massed paralysis, frantic
for any movement, for sheer outbreak of muscle.

RECOLLECTION AND VOCABULARY

There's an extra brightness on this side
that I wish to absorb, so I turn

my garnering sight into an opening
lightened by the yellowing of leaves;

what comes at me spills out of thimbles
of the world ill-fitting them; visualizing

and memorising canisters are overwhelmed
by the ordinary – (not excessive) – scene;

some words might be stained by the world,
or smells get caught in the phonetic fibres

of language; but not much of what I'm
walking through sticks really firm – it runs

off my surfaces, flows round my chosen words,
wastes itself helplessly into the unuttered past.

OMFG

My body makes that woman's
body three times demonic;
the cunning arrangement
of her features perplexes
my masculine insecurities;
the very fact of her sex
seems diabolical, testifying
to so much calculation,
to so much anticipation of
my most secret inclinations
that theology has to step in
to save me, using two naked
bodies and a garden to explain
exactly where I went wrong.

THE GREATEST POVERTY

I crave objects as spiky
as pineapples, as suave
as mangoes, objects that have
a career in engineering
or in sport, or catering.

They fit into each other
or into me, with a surgical
purpose or just for a laugh.
Their parentage is as various
as birth canals. The hook

on the end of a wasp's
foot is an object I love;
how hard-working they are,
humble as ball bearings.

SONGS

An especially vocal Scottish bird,
a linguist, is speaking in African –
birds in Botswana would understand
nae bother; how dry and lacquered
its hard voice is, as if composed
of polished beak and shiny nail.

Song-toads speak a soft universal tongue
in anything that qualifies as a swamp.

Blue bog-myrtle keeps its own
counsel, is never willing to bring
into play the powerful voice
muscles that are bunched under
its leaf armpits like sweat glands
or goiters the size of grapefruit.

SATISFACTION AND SATIATION

A lion shakes blood
from his prey-drenched
beard – red gore sprays
from sanguinous jaws;

stunned by repletion
the diner rocks back
in his chair – dull eyes
roll in a slow skull;

the sated swan lets
his bird-pizzle flop
out of the vagina
of the Greek woman;

slack chops hang,
dripping slather.
The world is dead.

DIRECT CURRENT

Putting my tongue to the terminals
for the salty shock of battery charge –
that is what is invited by the near-
spaces of the woman, her intimate
enclosure, when you are near enough
to hear and smell her, feel her static,
her vibrancy and radiation, radicals
of neck and shoulder, soul active
on her face, her odours as natural,
earthy, as root, swede and radish;
like an astronaut in zero gravity,
detached, focussed, but upside-down,
I feel the inverse world of her sex,
charged-particle pull and flow of her.

FALSE TEETH AND HEARING AIDS

Let the over-statements of her body,
her mispronouncements of weight
and age, her body's views coming out
in phonetic spillages of language,
let all that be placed in copper scales
balanced by hard grammes of brass —

you can love that over-indulgence,
the many years of chocolate and childbirth,
these are the eyes and hooks of attachment,
deviations from the tedium
of perfection, the narcoleptic pinnacles
of beauty; take her bunioned feet,

her lopsided breasts and faded irises,
and fold into acts of brutally honest sex.

ODE TO INDUSTRIAL BODIES

"You're such a loyal person,"
he said, giving her a big hug;
he loved women, perhaps
on account of their vaginas,
which were gods to him, the last
divinities left on earth.

Above the uterus, gleaming
like the chrome exhaust pipes
on American dragsters, were
the conception chambers,
suggestive of trumpets or tulips,
where new humans fruited.

Inside her throat, exhalations
were throttled into language.

ON THE AUTISM SPECTRUM

Faces reach me unmollified, their pure
psychiatry as raw as neat cane spirits;
they have slipped in still undrinkable,
without being boiled or watered down,
containing larvae, pests, bacteria, bits;
they are rough, unworked ores dug
straight from the earth, carrying
their original fierce mineral natures;
nothing shields me from their isotopes;
she looks at me, her face unearthed,
uninsulated, her copper wires exposed.
Geiger readings click over her bronze
materials, storms of radio messages
deliver at unbearable cosmic dosages.

FRENCH SAXOPHONE

A tenor saxophone traces
the graceful genetic curves
of its mass-production, from
the pinched mouthpiece to
its bell opening like a lily;
it is both a perfect copy
compliant with the house-style
of the Paris workshop where
it was crafted, and a template
for future saxophones
aspiring to silver parabolas
of metal lines; its gallic pedigree
shows in the bony profile,
the golden machinery of keys.

A POND OF LILIES

These outrageous plants can experiment
with lascivious shapes, shameless forms
that would be obscene if realised in flesh,
in animal bodies; sex organs take up 90%
of their surface areas, to the detriment
of their utility systems – eating is done
under water, or with the mouth stuffed
into soil; composed of expressionless
vegetable matter, they can perform
sexual intercourse right out in the open,
ejaculating with expletives of lust
in their silent floral language – decadent
royals, unabashed by a peeping clitoris
or hard erection prodding silk breeches.

AN IMAGINED RESUMPTION

I kneel before you, then crouch to kiss
my thanks onto your grubby feet,
as much for what has taken place over
the years, as for what's occurring now;

the female heart is a deep, forgiving
organ, always willing to entertain full
acquittals in its roomy chambers;
but the resumption of our marine
secrecy is a big ask — that you consent

to hang your naked breasts over the waist-
band of your skirt while I play about
in the oystery saltiness of your sex;
and that I be allowed to suck the soft
octopus of your vagina into my mouth.

CLEAN AND BUSY SEAS

Waters awash with krill
froth at the mouth;
fish and other oceanic
concoctions enjoy their
marine-salt preservations;
single sheets of sardines,
their backs to the sun,
slide within their layers
of pelagic shallows;
paradise is oh so close,
sharing precious space
with sting-rays, bleached
white utopias, derelict
seas floating belly-up.

CREEK FISHING

Everything is identical right until
the creature breaks from the water –
lagoon, creek or narcotic river,
rods flexed over golden sleep;

nylon lines are gently tautened
to carry signals of motion
from that world to this, along
almost invisible, glinting pulses;

even the splash and the strike
are the same on each occasion,
willow-bend of tight parabola,

furious playing-out and reeling in;
and then the animal sails out –
the secret body of the wetness.

POTABLE GOLD

By the time it has reached us
it's cheerful – see how it chafes
a glow into brickwork and tile;
we picture, then, its smiling
origin, roughly two hours away
as given by the speed of light –
a benign and beaming countenance.

What a travesty of the fanatical
hydrogen-burner way out there –
a solar brute which vaporises
everything within its reach,
dropping brand new elements
out of its fires like boiled glass;
look no further for hell itself.

THE SUPPLIANTS

Now the imploring vines stretch
halfway up and across my window,
begging to be let in, to be given
what I have, to share my shelter,
to sit at my table and write poetry
as I do, to eat in my way, the decent
and the human way, with hands
and a mouth, with the upper half
of my body, and not be like them
having to sit with their lower halves
buried up to the waist in ripe
garden muck, battering their stems
on my window and having to suck
food up through their arseholes.

SUSANNAH SOILED

The Elders poke their nosey parkers
over the hedge – their dirty looks
are hooded beneath eyelids as fleshy
as foreskins; Suzannah is bathing
en plein air, in flagrant dereliction
of good sense; there she is, a naked
babe recoiling from the soiling eyes
of the old men focusing all their
spare brain capacity on her pink
blushes; even the artist is astounded
by what his artistry can achieve –
half-mesmerised, he lets his brushes
show him where to stroke, to pause,
to stroke, pause, stroke her into life.

THE WORLD AS WILL

New ivy shoots crowd against the glass
like children; did Schopenhauer imply
that we are guardians of the natural world
or have I misunderstood that? In any case
the responsibility is misplaced; I am not
some kind father to these imploring growths
tapping their desires on my window pane;
blinder than moles burrowing through
an impalpable soil of light and air, feeling
their way forward like sightless men – masters
of their own fate they emphatically are not;
we are all cast up here by force of climate,
compost, biological muscle. My brethren,
keep me company on this stricken planet.

CROW THEOLOGY

Every crow is a gifted metaphysician
with leanings towards the priesthood;
disputation is second nature to them;
they are born with doctrinal dogmas
already formed in their brains, best seen
to advantage at theology conventions
in the quadrangles of higher learning;
they philosophise with built-in Motorola
64-bit processors, arguments ready-
formed in their Read Only Memories,
which is the crow-equivalent of DNA.
What they don't know about the Bible
isn't worth knowing; their crow-logic
flummoxes every academic opponent.

MY NEFERTITI

When she comes she howls
like a flogged Russian peasant;
she turns me into a boyar,
a landowner of the steppes
abusing his sharecroppers;
she is my African woman,
my Black, rousing colonial
lust and greed as I make
her body do certain things
at the limits of its nature;
a slave owner, I drive her
to this proletarian outcry –
my dark Nubian woman,
my brown-eyed Bedouin.

VEGETABLE NATURE ONE VAST PARASITE

Paralysed from the twiglets down,
all botanical behaviour is passive,
a mechanism of suction and pressure
imposed on nerveless, non-muscular
tubes; gravity and osmosis knead
the wristfuls of conduits packed
inside trunks and stems; moisture
rises by application of basic Matric
physics to a porous medium dipped
in wet soil and compost; our modest
household plant sends it roots to sleep
in garden muck, and resigns itself to
a life of penury and vegetable sloth.
Time and Boyle's Law do all the rest.

WORKING-CLASS JESUS

I'm here to talk about our
Lord's working-class roots,
his well-known predilection
for carpenters, fishermen,
con-men and sex offenders –
more at home with grafters
and graspers, time servers
and ne'er-do-wells, than with
magistrates, bankers, parsons
and the squeaky clean, always
ready to leave his good flock
stranded halfway up a prayer
while he went in search of
some slapper on the skids.

DREAMED IN STERTOROUS SLEEP

sunflower oil – light yellow compress –
    oleagenous, thinly fragrant
    crushed from black pips;
extraction – a human (collective) trait –
    wells and derricks
    a willingness to imitate;
transformation – chymical investigations
    leaning heavily to sorcery
    and brutal cuisines;
dispelting – deshanking, deadheading,
    wrongfooting, bowelstitching,
    dismembering and broiling;
vegetable oil – seed oil, nut oil, bean oil,
    a pure botanical fixation
    to cleanse the palate.

AFTERWORD to Playing with My Christianity

Playing with My Christianity is the second volume in what was planned to be an exhaustive three-volume collection of the roughly 600 small-scale poems ("sonnets") that I wrote between 2011 and 2019 in the Edinburgh University Main Library. However, having looked more critically at the 400 poems remaining after the publication of Volume One (*Gathering Photons in May*), I decided that the standard of some of them did not justify two whole further volumes. I have therefore decided to limit myself to just one more volume (the current one) containing the best of the remaining poems.

I see the poems in this collection as short journeys through matter, brief excursions into the material world; they carry the reader into a portion of that world, and then out the other side, in the hope that this journey will affect them pleasurably or provokingly for a brief period. These poems are thus experiences before they are meanings.

In many instances the poems in this gathering run on the smell of an oil-rag – they don't use high-octane fuels (political, or whatever) to drive them along.

It's true that I do sometimes have bones to pick with religion, capitalism, planet-despoliation, and a few other pressing matters; but more characteristically the aesthetic I treasure most is one expressed by John Cage in this trenchant paradox: "I have nothing to say, and I'm saying it, and that is poetry" (from *Silence*).

What this signifies in my case is that I treat the subject-matter of my poems as just one rhetorical device among many, on a par with imagery, alliteration or punctuation. It doesn't really matter what the poem is about, or even that it's about anything at all – the purpose of the poem's subject-matter is to give it a certain narrative momentum, rather than to be the ground of its moral or philosophical *raison d'être*. There can never be too many poems about Staffordshire Terriers, for example, so long as the poems are radical, risk-taking, energetic and quick. Sceptics may wish to refer to Norman MacCaig's "Seen in the City" for confirmation of this.

OUTSIDER ART

Because a fair proportion of the sonnets in this volume are non-thematic in this way, there is indeed an occasional repetitiveness of subject-matter – variety is supplied by differences of season, hour, light, atmosphere, mood and dogma, and so on. There is an analogy here with what is sometimes referred to as Outsider Art, art made by and for people "on the autism spectrum." My favourite example is that of a certain landscape artist who would set himself up in exactly the same spot in the same park every day of the year, and paint exactly the same scene over and over, with little beyond botanical and weather variations to tell one painting from another. The result, en masse, was captivating. If any of my poems were to be described as a product of both autism and artistry, I would not be offended by that observation.

ALPHABETICAL INDEX

A Common Road	138
A Descent of Man	153
A Food Amnesty	23
A Glans Sonnet	139
A Glass Sonnet	39
A Pond of Lilies	188
A Posy of Smells	170
A Pragmatic Crow	55
A Question for The Dawn	118
A Second Human	5
A Solo Wedding in Kyoto	59
A Stoic's Injunction	130
A Tale from Ovid	69
A Woman of Years	125
Aargh!	77
Acid Recall	53
Adrenalin	8
Ages of Apogees	94
Albertine Asleep	140
Albuminous Squid	45
Amplification	103
An Ambivalent Bequest	98
An Imagined Resumption	189
An Insect of the Order Odonata	56
At the Mercy	131
Atrophy and Regeneration	85
Beef Cheeks and Cauliflower	41
Bird Feeders to The Rescue	149
Brain Habitat	33
Bright Stipplings	11
Bulawayo Sex Lessons	99

Cardiomyopathy	119
Clarinet Dropsy in Dalmeny Kirk	159
Clean And Busy Seas	190
Close to Perfection	58
Cold And Crows	132
Comparative Religion	133
Concrete Dipping Basin	72
Country Proverbs	76
Creek Fishing	191
Crow Landing	86
Crow Theology	196
Crows Clowning in the Air	36
David Hockney's Arrival of Spring	54
Dead Musical Trees	82
Descriptive Limits	30
Dialect Of the Tribe	142
Direct Current	183
Dreamed In Stertorous Sleep	200
Dromedaris, Reijger, Goede Hoop	101
Earth-Collapse	9
Eating Squid	52
Elizabethan Love Sonnet	3
Engine Philology	89
English in Africa	108
Ennui	29
Exactly Ten O'clock	37
Exercise Regime	121
Expunged	150
Eyeballed by an Ant	28
False Teeth and Hearing Aids	184
Field Naturalist in Situ	167
First Thing	166
Fishes in Books	106
Fit as a Fly	40

Flight Readiness	32
Flip-Flop	115
Flushing Out the Game	12
Forces on Phrasal Structure	84
French Saxophone	187
Full Immersive Response	135
Gigolo	120
Homunculus	127
I Have Read *Watt*	123
Ice	44
Impulse and Direction	2
In A French Field	143
In a Hide	122
In His Own Image	27
In The Thread of Compte	175
In/Out	110
Initiation Rapture	172
Japanese Dagger	107
John Ruskin, *Blenheim Orange Apple*	34
Landing A Shit-House on The Moon	117
Leafing Creeper	79
Lessons from a Native	96
Lessons in Baroque Decorum	92
Library Session 531	163
Life Brought into the House	134
Like A South-Facing Window	176
Living On the Moon	169
Lock Up Your Drawers	57
Love Among the Over-Sixties	97
Lunar Theatre	161
Measures	162
Mere Heavenly Walking	171
Metatarsus Varies	141
Mists and Fruitfulness	100

Mortarless Cities of Central Africa	155
Mother and Daughter	63
My Nefertiti	197
My Penitential Greens	24
Native Language Landscape	18
Native To the Islands	112
Naughty Greens	16
Navigation in Green Water	129
Not Such a Pathetic Fallacy	91
Ode To Industrial Bodies	185
OMFG	179
On My Late Espoused Saint	46
On The Autism Spectrum	186
On the Train to Fish Hoek	78
Ordinance Lost Overboard	158
Our Personal Moons	4
Out of the Forcing-Box	80
Palliatives for a Tormented Parliament	66
Pamela In Her Body	157
Performative Utterance	88
Persuasion	17
Playing with My Christianity	71
Pleiade	114
Poet To Social Worker	174
Politics of a Dutiful Daughter	26
Potable Gold	192
Power	47
Raw Philosophy of Miracles	152
Readers of God	68
Recollection and Vocabulary	178
Return From the Islands	126
Right Ventricular Cardiomyopathy	102
Rough Gully Bash	168
Satisfaction And Satiation	182

Seasonal Euphoria	35
Seceding Embodiment	42
Seeing Quince	70
Shatterproof	43
Shoes In the Charity Shop	164
Sleeping Swans	31
Snap	38
Soft Enough to Eat	64
Solar Alchemies	156
Songs	181
Sonnet Hornet	22
Sound-Creep	73
Spelt	95
Spirals	14
Spring Epidemiology	20
Star Traveller	61
Steeped in World	25
Stiff and Salty Boots	60
Still Morning with Birdflight	177
Stone World	145
Susannah Soiled	194
Suspicions Of the Ancestral Ape	151
Tales From Plutarch	62
Talkin' 'Bout My Generation	87
Tangled In the Metaphysics of Time	111
Tarmac and Tapestry	21
The Common People	124
The Concept of Nature	146
The Difference	10
The Earth Our Dwelling Place	147
The Fierce Wheat in Samuel Palmer	160
The Fly Is a Perfect Example	75
The Grass Campaigns	154
The Greatest Poverty	180

The Illusion Room	128
The Locust Daughters	93
The Pleasures of Reading	113
The Real Work	116
The Suppliants	193
The Vagina	50
The World as Will	195
This Object	15
Thousand Year Reigns	165
Time's Numbering Clock	67
Tranny	48
Transmission	83
Trumpet Raspberry	19
Tutti	105
Uit Die Hantam	148
Understanding Poetry	1
Urban Igloo	109
Vanishing Apes	137
Vegetable Nature One Vast Parasite	198
Visibly Touched	7
Voyages of Discovery	104
Weapons of the Friendly Isles	136
Weather Masters	13
Wedding Cemetery	144
Well-Earned Growth Rings	51
Who Was the Prophet's Mother?	173
Wilkinson Sword	81
Winged and Wonderful	65
Woman Reclining on a Leopard Skin	49
Working-Class Jesus	199
Writing	6
Writing for the Mouth	90
Yeah! Yeah! Yeah!	74

Milton Keynes UK
Ingram Content Group UK Ltd.
UKHW011824131023
430526UK00004B/237